"In *This is Living!* Bettina Schuller guides us through worship where the skeptics, non-believers, and unaffiliated are welcomed with the same generosity of spirit as the most devout congregants and clergy. I came away from *This is Living!* with a fresh appreciation that everyday prayer in its elemental form is as vital to human life as breathing."

—David Henry, *Los Angeles Times* bestselling author of
Furious Cool: Richard Pryor and the World That Made Him.

"The cacophony of our fast paced world often drowns out the symphony of God's voice. In *This is Living! Practicing the Presence of God,* Bettina Schuller combines science, history, spirituality, personal anecdote and practical prayer instruction to help us slow down and hear God's voice and experience God's presence. This book deserves a place of daily companionship with you on your journey through life!"

—The Right Reverend Dabney T. Smith
Bishop, Episcopal Diocese of Southwest Florida

"Bettina Schuller speaks from stillness. Her book is a guide on how to discover the extraordinary in the ordinary and live in the presence of God. *This is Living!* is a "must have" for everyone's daily reading."

—Ann M. Douglas, author and illustrator of
Freddy & Flossy Flutterby

"I have never felt so simultaneously inspired and peaceful as I did while reading *This is Living!* Rooted in Christianity but accessible to those of every faith, this book provides spiritual guidance for both everyday tasks and deep self-healing. I would recommend this to anyone on a quest for a more fulfilled life."

—Joan Johnston, *New York Times* bestselling author

THIS IS LIVING!

This is Living!

Practicing the Presence of God

*A Prayer and Meditation Guide
for Daily Life*

BETTINA SCHULLER

Cover design by Carolin Proeger; wearesgnl.com

Cover image by Gina White; visualpoetrybygina.com

Editing by Maya Trevathan; mayaunmarketed.com

Printed by CreateSpace, an Amazon.com Company
First printing 2017

ISBN-13: 978-1976460562
ISBN-10: 1976460565

Library of Congress Control Number: 2017914571
CreateSpace Independent Publishing Platform, North Charleston, SC

To my daughters, Maya and Sophia

For Caroline,
With appreciation for
you and your
authentic spiritual
journey,
Bethine

Listen to your life.
See it for the fathomless mystery it is.
In the boredom and pain of it
no less than in the excitement and gladness:
touch, taste, smell your way
to the holy and hidden heart of it
because in the last analysis
all moments are key moments,
and life itself is grace.

—Frederick Buechner

CONTENTS

PREFACE

When I read Brother Lawrence's *Practicing the Presence of God* for the first time, I was fascinated and wanted to learn how to live with an awareness of God's presence in all I do, and do it all for the glory of God. I knew how to pray unceasingly by praying Breath Prayers, Prayers of the Heart and sitting in Centering Prayer. It wasn't what I understood as "practicing the presence of God," though. I wanted to learn how to "turn the cake that is frying on the pan for the love of Him," as Brother Lawrence describes in one of his letters. I yearned to know God's presence while I folded the laundry and how to wake up in the morning with God's love in my heart. But I did not find any instructions in Brother Lawrence's beautiful 17th-century writings. I was looking for prayers that were easily integrated into the day, prayers that would help me put the concept of practicing the presence of God into action. I discovered that if I wanted to pray this way and help others do the same, I had to pray and write these prayers into life. And that is what I did! I have based the Prayers of Presence on Brother Lawrence's writings about practicing the presence of God.

I chose the subtitle in honor of Brother Lawrence, whose letters, conversations and spiritual maxims were translated and compiled into a book by many different authors and called either *The Practice of the Presence of God* or *Practicing the Presence of God*. I chose the subtitle *Practicing the Presence of God* because praying the Prayers of Presence is an ongoing process. Practicing the presence of God requires an understanding of God that goes beyond the "practice" of God. Richard Rohr, a contemporary Franciscan priest, describes it beautifully in his book *The Naked Now*: "At this point, God becomes more a verb than a noun, more a process than a conclusion, more an experience than a dogma, more a personal relationship than an idea."[1]

I pray that the Prayers of Presence will help you discover God's ever-present love and peace in your life. At the deepest level of your being, you are always praying!

INTRODUCTION

I am sitting on a small island in one of the big Canadian lakes, looking out onto the glassy surface of the water. The sun is peeking through the big red pine on my left, my dog Joy is lying at my feet, and I hear the faint noise of what might be an airplane. Birds are chirping, a hummingbird is flying to the red flower on my right and the occasional drip of water reminds me of the stormy rain last night.

PRAYING PAUSE

> *Where are you sitting?... Relax your body into the chair or couch... Look at your surroundings... Listen for a moment... Rest in the softness and rhythm of your breathing.*

Since you have picked up this book, you are likely someone who is on a spiritual path and who would like to know more about prayer and God's presence in your life. You might also be a person who has not had a relationship with the Divine, who does not know how to pray and who would like to connect with a power greater than yourself. No matter your spiritual background, the Prayers of Presence may be unfamiliar and might not even feel like prayer at first. Most of us are used to praying with words, petitioning God and thanking God. We might know how to say, "Thy will be done," but do we know how to listen to the answer? God speaks to us in many different ways: the Bible, worship, nature, other people, our life situations and stillness. This book is about experiencing God moment by moment in ourselves, in other living beings and while we are living our day-to-day life. It is about experiencing the extraordinary in the ordinary, the Holy in the midst of life.

Most of us have a name for the life force that lies beyond our own life. Whatever word we use, whether we prefer "God," "Divine Power," "Higher Power," "Presence of the Universe," "Being" or "I AM," let us not get hung up on words. These prayers go beyond that. If we take words literally and think we know the truth behind them, we might get stuck in ideas and theories and miss God altogether.

PRAYING PAUSE

> *Rest in your breathing for a moment... Your mind*
> *wants to go on reading but God might want you*
> *to come into the present moment... Look up from*
> *this book and look at your surroundings...*
> *Choose a favorite painting, object or plant and*
> *look at it with no agenda... Let the beauty of it*
> *touch your soul for a while... Feel God's presence*

*in the "here and now" and the place you are in... It
is holy ground because God is in it and you are in
God!*

You just prayed a Prayer of Presence by being aware
of yourself and your surroundings. Is it as simple as
this? YES! It is this simple and still not easy at all.

My faith lies in a God who is "I AM" (Exodus 3:14
NIV), which means present every moment of my life. I
want to deepen my relationship with God who is "I AM"
not only in designated times of worship and prayer; I
want to learn how to live in the presence of God.

I am blessed to have known a person who lived in
God's presence every moment of his later life. Simon
Schuller was 90 years old when I met him at the
Cleveland airport for the first time. Although already
slow and unsteady in his walking, he insisted on
meeting me at the gate. He welcomed me in my native
language with a big smile and a hug, joyfully shouting,
"This is Living!" Throughout the next four years that I
had God's grace of knowing him, I heard him gratefully
shout "This is Living!" many, many times. Whether it
was over a cup of steaming coffee, a beautiful flower, a
crescent moon or simply the breaths he took, Si was
aware of God and always celebrated that presence with
his joyful catchphrase. The night Simon Schuller died,
he came to me in a dream and let me know that,
ultimately, "*This* is Living!"

As a spiritual director and retreat leader, I teach contemplative prayer at churches, retreat centers and during spiritual direction. Many of the retreatants come because they want a closer connection with God. They know intellectually that God is always with them, but do not feel God's presence in their daily lives. Many of them want to practice contemplative prayer, but do not find the time for a regular practice and give it up altogether. The questions

"How can I become aware of God's presence during the day?"

"How can I integrate God into my life in all I do?"

"How can I pray during the day?"

"I have read The Practice of the Presence of God *by Brother Lawrence but I don't know how to do it. He doesn't really give any prayer instructions. How can I practice the presence of God?"*

were asked many times during retreats and spiritual direction. I finally was persuaded that I had to share my experience by writing down the Prayers of Presence. I certainly didn't plan to write a book, but here I am! I am not a native English speaker and since there are so many books already published on prayer, I asked myself if I really had something new to say. After a time of discernment and prayer, I could answer my question with "Yes." I was called to write a book that would help people feel God's presence during the day without adding yet another time commitment to it.

Spiritual leaders in other faith traditions and leaders in the medical community have written books about the importance and physical benefits of living in the present moment. Thich Nhat Han, Eckhart Tolle, Jack Kornfield, Jon Kabat-Zinn and others have shared insights and meditations from the perspective of their faith traditions and belief systems. The Christian Contemplative movement has renewed and rediscovered old traditional practices like Lectio Divina and Centering Prayer in the last 50 years. Father Thomas Keating, a Trappist monk and one of the founders of the Centering Prayer movement, talks about the importance of extending the effects of Centering Prayer into daily life. It was Brother Lawrence, though, and the yearning of my friends and retreatants who inspired and encouraged me to write a book about living in the present moment with God.

In Contemplative circles, we hear that we have to "be" instead of "do" and I could not agree more wholeheartedly. Our society is geared toward doing; the more we do, the more we are admired and rewarded. And yet stress related illnesses are on a steep rise. It seems that we have to relearn to "be," or our health will suffer tremendously. What if we combined "being" with "doing"? What if we could practice God's presence in all we do, as Brother Lawrence suggests, and connect with God's depth and soul in our daily lives? My hope is that the Prayers of Presence will bring the teachings of Brother Lawrence into a practical context in your life and help you to be present with God moment by moment. Since we have to "do," we might as well "be" while we "do."

Here are a few suggestions for your journey through this book. I have written it in such a way that you can read it from cover to cover, or read one chapter and skip the next. You can just read the prayers and skip the first part, if that is right for you. We all have a unique relationship with God and we need to honor this uniqueness and acknowledge that what is right for you might not be right for me.

Part One, "The Fundamentals of the Prayers of Presence," provides the theological background for the prayers within the history of the Christian church, offers some neurological research and shares the psychological and emotional effects of the prayers. The chapter "Practicing the Prayers of Presence" talks about how to allow and accept God's guidance in all situations of our lives.

Part Two introduces the Prayers of Presence. The forty prayers are divided into Breath Prayers, Body Awareness Prayers and Daily Awareness Prayers. The separation is somewhat artificial because most of the prayers overlap into two or even three categories. It is the main focus of each prayer that determined which category I chose.

The quotations throughout the book are from contemporary writers, unless indicated otherwise.

The "Praying Pauses" integrated throughout the book ask you to take a break from the intellectual activity of reading and to become aware of the present moment. The meditations and questions asked in the "Praying Pauses" connect you with your life experience and spiritual journey. They teach you as much or more as the text about "Practicing the Presence of God." You connect with God on a deeper level if you spend as much time pausing for prayer as reading this book.

PRAYING PAUSE

> *Rest softly in the rhythm of your breathing... Feel the air coming into your body and leaving your body... Are you ready to experience God in a new way?... Are you willing to let this praying process change your life into a life of Presence?*

Choosing to pray — and it doesn't matter how — is making a commitment to experience God. No matter what form of prayer we choose, one thing is for certain: We learn to pray by praying and not by talking or reading about prayer! Practicing the presence of God by praying "unceasingly" is your part in the spiritual journey toward God, and God takes care of the rest.

This book and these prayers are written in the spirit of simplicity. Everyone who chooses to pray this way can do it. There is no right or wrong and there are no specific rules to follow. All you need is your breath, your body and your daily life to learn how to pray this way.

PART I

THE FUNDAMENTALS OF THE PRAYERS OF PRESENCE

Jesus said, "You examine the face of heaven and earth, but you have not come to know the one who is in your presence, and you do not know how to examine the moment."
—Coptic Gospel of Thomas #3

The Christian Foundation of the Prayers of Presence

Spirituality is not to be learned by flight from the world, or by running away from things, or by turning solitary and going apart from the world. Rather, we must learn an inner solitude wherever or with whomsoever we may be. We must learn to penetrate things and find God there.
—Meister Eckhart (1260-1327)

The purpose of this book is to offer practical prayers for your daily life to help you find the inner solitude the Christian mystic Meister Eckhart is talking about. It is less about theological concepts and ideas. However, it is still necessary for many of us to put spiritual concepts that are new to us into known Christian context. The theological background for the Prayers of Presence is *Practicing the Presence of God* by Brother Lawrence.

Praying Pause

Take a minute and look into yourself... Are you a person who would benefit from knowing the theological background?... Or are you a person who learns better by jumping in right away and experiencing the prayers?... There is no right or wrong. The important thing is to do what works best for you.

The concept of worshiping God throughout the day is not new. It has existed within Christianity from its very beginning. Brother Lawrence's approach of practicing the presence of God in all we do is only one example of the richness and diversity of Christian worship. Saints and mystics like The Desert Fathers and Mothers, Meister Eckhart, St. Julian of Norwich, St. Teresa of Avila, Thomas Merton, and many others throughout history have beautifully revealed the depth of the Christian tradition of an ever-present God, but it was Brother Lawrence who inspired me to write this book.

Brother Lawrence is known for his spiritual teachings that promoted awareness of God's presence in day-to-day living. He felt God's presence in everyday tasks and worshiped God in all he did. Whether he prayed at a designated time, made a meal or wrote a letter, he did it with the assurance that God was with him and that he was with God.

Brother Lawrence's spiritual teachings are the theological basis for the Prayers of Presence. I will do my best to bring his teachings closer to you in this chapter. I write, "do my best" because, as simple as his spiritual teachings are, they are difficult to understand since they are mainly to be experienced and not analyzed by the mind. As I mentioned in the introduction, I have integrated "Praying Pauses" throughout the chapter so you can meditate on his teachings and apply them to your own spiritual life. The pauses will help you to experience Brother Lawrence's teachings. A friend of mine once told me she has tried to read *Practicing the Presence of God* many times, but cannot make it to the end because "he loses me along the way." Another friend wondered where in his book Brother Lawrence explains how to practice the presence of God. It is my hope to shed some light on Brother Lawrence and his spiritual practice and to provide prayers for practicing his teachings in Part Two of this book.

Brother Lawrence's work consists of letters to his spiritual friends and the wisdom he shared with Father Joseph De Beaufort, counsel to the Archbishop of Paris. He never wrote a book, or even intended for any of his writings to be published. In fact, he made it very clear to "Reverend Mother N." not to share any of his writings:

"Since you have expressed such an eager desire to have me share with you the method I have used to arrive at that state of the presence of God ... I cannot conceal from you that it is with great reluctance that I allow myself to be won over by your persistence. I am writing only under the condition that you will not share my letter with anyone."[1]

Father Joseph De Beaufort had heard about the brother's unusual wisdom and met with him in 1666. Brother Lawrence granted Cardinal De Beaufort four interviews after he had reassured himself that the interest was genuine and not politically motivated. We know these interviews today as "The Conversations," in which Brother Lawrence describes his way of life and his relationship with God. De Beaufort publicized those conversations along with the letters after Brother Lawrence's death in 1691. The letters were written in the last ten years of Brother Lawrence's life.

Nicholas Herman — who later became Brother Lawrence — was born in France into a peasant family in 1611. He joined the army, as many poor young men did then, but at the age of 18, Herman had a profound contemplative experience that changed the course of his life. It was not a supernatural vision, which many saints described in those days but a moment of clarity that he had never before experienced. When Herman looked at a barren tree in the winter, stripped of leaves and fruit, he suddenly realized that the tree, though barren at the moment, would again bear fruit in the summer. He knew it on the level of his mind but at that moment it reached a depth that he had not known before. He experienced the miracle of life. Herman who himself felt barren at that moment, knew that by the grace of God, he would bear fruit in the future as well. He experienced God's presence right there and then as a living truth.

Six years after this contemplative experience, Herman entered the Discalced Carmelite monastery in Paris and became Brother Lawrence of the Resurrection. Later in life Brother Lawrence shared his belief that this type of moment can happen to anyone, and that we are all capable of living this way.

PRAYING PAUSE

Take a few conscious breaths... Do you remember a contemplative experience in your life, a moment where you suddenly felt God's truth in a new way? It might have been an experience in nature, with a loved one or an event during which you suddenly saw the truth of something more clearly. Close your eyes and go into the details of it; see, hear, smell, touch and feel the moment again with your whole being...

Do you feel it is possible to share this experience adequately with words?

Brother Lawrence, who could read and write but was not well educated, was assigned to work in the monastery kitchen for most of his life. Although he disliked kitchen work, he remained content where he was and with what he did: "The time of business does not with me differ from the time of prayer; and in the noise and clatter of my kitchen, while several persons are at the same time calling for different things, I possess God in as great tranquility as if I were upon my knees at the blessed sacrament."[2]

Brother Lawrence emanated such deep peace and tranquility that many people came to the monastery to seek his spiritual guidance. He taught that prayer is not only something one engages in at specific times during the day. His spiritual gift to us is the notion that our whole life can be prayer. This truth can be lived by anyone, regardless of age or life circumstance, and is as applicable today as it was four hundred years ago because the prayer material is our day-to-day life.

Let's look at some of Brother Lawrence's spiritual insights to be able to understand what he means by "practicing the presence of God" in all we do. First, let's examine Brother Lawrence's relationship with God. For him, God is part of our soul and we are part of God: "He is within us. Seek Him not elsewhere."[3]

PRAYING PAUSE

Rest in your breathing for a moment... Imagine the ocean and its relationship to the waves... Meditate on this image for a while... If it is helpful, draw it, write about it, watch a video of

*the ocean or look at a picture of it; go to the
ocean if you live near it. As always, take your
time and experience this pause rather than read
on and feed your mind... God can only be
experienced and not understood!*

God is the ocean and we are the waves. On a
cognitive level, we understand what the ocean is, what
the waves are, and how they are related. It is already a
blessing if we understand the closeness of our
relationship with God on this mental level. However, if
we stay on this level, we do not progress from the
theoretical idea of God to the spiritual experience
because "God is beyond our understanding."[4] It is an
experience that requires delving deeper into ourselves.

Let's stay with our metaphor of the ocean and go
beyond our understanding. How could somebody
explain to us what water feels like, smells like, and
sounds like? How could somebody explain what water
feels like on our skin after we have been in the hot sun
for too long? How could somebody explain what salt
water on our body feels and tastes like? How could
somebody possibly explain what it feels like to dive into
the water and feel the weightlessness of our body as we
swim in the ocean? If we love the ocean, how could we
possibly understand somebody's fear of it?

PRAYING PAUSE

What does it mean to you to know God through love and to understand God beyond words?... Sit in silence for a while, rest in the rhythm of your breathing and remember a time when you experienced God through love...

My personal experience of times when I knew God through love were experiences with both my daughters. These experiences were something I did every day but somehow through God's grace, these particular ones were holy and I felt the One Love. The first one was with my older daughter. I nursed Maya one night, as I did every night, and it seemed like Maya and I were the only people awake in the world. Looking down at her, I experienced the miracle of life and love beyond words. I felt God in us and all around us. Another time was with my daughter Sophia. I took my sleeping baby gently out of the car seat and she looked briefly up at me, cuddling into my arms with trust and total surrender, knowing she was safe and held with love. I knew God through love right then and there. God was holding me the same way as I did my baby. Although these words do not do justice to the experience I had, I wanted to share these beautiful experiences. They opened my eyes to God's love in the way that the "barren tree experience" did for Brother Lawrence.

Not only can we experience God through love, but also by faith. Brother Lawrence writes, "...by Faith I learn more of God, and in a very little time, than I could do in the schools after many a long year."[5]

PRAYING PAUSE

Have you ever learned more of God by faith? Can you remember when you acted on faith and you realized that faith was all you had to make a decision? Could we call faith our intuition? Do we follow God when we follow our intuition instead of our rational mind?... Do you remember a time when you acted on faith?

When I left Germany to move to the United States at the age of thirty, I think I went on faith, but I am not sure. My faith in God that it was the right decision was all I had to go on. But I also knew that I could go back to Germany if it didn't work out. So have I ever known God by faith? To be honest, I am not really sure... Brother Lawrence tells us that if we live and pray in the presence of God, our faith will come alive. It will become so alive "...that the soul can almost say – Faith is swallowed up in Sight, I see and I experience."[6]

Living by faith is a difficult concept. To live by faith requires giving up control ("Thy will be done," as in the Lord's Prayer), knowing that one is not in charge of one's life, and totally surrendering to a power that the mind doesn't even "know" exists.

If we want to practice the presence of God as Brother Lawrence taught, we have to live by faith that God is within and around us, and that we live in God's presence at all times. We also need to be willing to open our hearts and get to know God through love. Brother Lawrence writes, "In the depths of our soul, God reveals Himself, could we but realize it, yet we will not look there for Him."[7] If God lives in the depths of our soul, we have to get to know ourselves and who we truly are. That leads us to the next step in our spiritual journey with Brother Lawrence: "When we enter upon the spiritual life, we ought to consider thoroughly what we are, probing to the very depth."[8]

Most people identify themselves with the roles they occupy in life and the thoughts they have about themselves; for example, "I am a mother," "I am a teacher," or "I am a bad cook," etc. We are not our roles though, nor our thoughts! Our thoughts about ourselves, others and life tend to come and go. One moment we might have a positive thought about ourselves and our life, yet the next moment we could shift gears and have negative thoughts about those same things. Thoughts constantly change. The essence of "I am" is the consciousness that is aware of our thoughts. The following meditation might help you to experience this consciousness.

PRAYING PAUSE

*Sit comfortably and rest in the rhythm of your
breathing for a moment... Now put your
awareness into listening... What do you hear?...
Listen for a moment... Now become aware of your
breathing for a moment... While you were aware
of what you heard, you were likely not aware of
your breath, and vice versa. However, you were
still breathing, or still hearing, without being
conscious of it. The presence behind all your
perceptions makes it possible for you to put your
awareness into different parts of your being. Also,
while you were aware of your breathing or what
you heard, you were likely unaware of your
thoughts... Try it again.*

To get to know God and ourselves, we need to
connect with this deeper presence within. Who is this
"I" that is able to be aware of thoughts, hearing, seeing,
smelling, feeling and breathing?

Brother Lawrence provides another important
insight regarding self-knowledge and closeness to God.
Writing of himself in the third person, he said, "He
never any longer thought ... on his past sins, nor on
those he daily committed, after he had asked God's
forgiveness of them."[9] We all make mistakes, and have
to claim responsibility for them. Brother Lawrence

expected himself to make mistakes since, "I shall never do otherwise, if I am left to myself."[10] As human beings, we are bound to err, and if we hold on to our mistakes and feel guilty, we put the guilt between God and us. All we have to do is own up to our missteps, make amends and let them go. Dwelling on our mistakes not only takes us away from the present moment, but can also negatively influence the decisions we make today. We get stuck in our spiritual journey if we are afraid to make mistakes, and consequently are not bold in our prayers and actions. It will paralyze us, for there is nothing worse for our spiritual growth than indecisiveness.

Let's be like Brother Lawrence and be able to say that, "By rising after my falls, and by frequently renewed acts of faith and love, I am come to a state wherein it would be as difficult for me not to think of God as it was at first to accustom myself to it."[11] Additionally, Brother Lawrence gave all the glory to God when he had done well in his work and life, saying that, "when he had finished, he examined himself how he had discharged his duty; if he found well, he returned thanks to God."[12]

PRAYING PAUSE

Become aware of your body... Soften your face...
Relax your jaw, shoulders and stomach... Breathe

deeply into your stomach area... God wants you to rest for a moment... Gently remember some of the mistakes you have made... You made them because you didn't know better or you wouldn't have made them... Let go and forgive yourself for being human... God has long forgiven you...

Living in the presence of God may sound difficult and overwhelming. In fact, it was not easy for Brother Lawrence to live this way at first. He spent years disciplining his heart and mind to yield to God's presence. De Beaufort tells us in the second conversation that, "...this trouble of mind lasted four years during which time he had suffered much."[13] In one of his letters, Brother Lawrence cautions someone who might have been impatient with the process of practicing the presence of God: "One does not become holy all at once."[14] This serves as a wonderful reminder for us to be patient and to persevere in our practice, so that we too can get to know God by faith.

PRAYING PAUSE

Do you know a person who exudes deep joy and peace?... There are people out there today who, like Brother Lawrence, live a quiet and unassuming life close to God. May be you could ask them about their journey with God...

If you have followed Brother Lawrence's spiritual teachings so far, and understand his spiritual maxims, you might be taken aback by his next statement: "Since you cannot but know that God is with you in all you undertake, that He is at the very depth and center of your soul, why should you not thus pause an instant from your outward business, and even in the act of prayer, to worship Him within your soul."[15]

This is how I understand it. When we worship God in all we do, we still have to focus on what we are actually doing, whether it is reading the Bible or doing the dishes. Some of our attention is needed to hold the Bible, or to get the dishes clean. Brother Lawrence tells us that there is a deeper level in us, the "depth and center of our soul" or "the depth of our being," where we can worship God. Even if we read the Bible or pray in words, Brother Lawrence wants us to stop and worship God. He wants us to come out of our head and into our heart, or, as we learn in the next chapter, switch from our left-brain hemisphere into our right. Brother Lawrence wants us to stop thinking about God and start loving God. He wants us to connect with God at a level that most of us have not yet experienced. But because he knows that it is impossible "to disregard completely and forever the outward things that are around us,"[16] he tells us the different steps we have to take to live in the presence of God. If we think about our relationship with God as the ocean and the waves, we might understand that Brother Lawrence wants our consciousness to completely leave the wave once in a while and flow into the vastness of the ocean.

Practicing the presence of God is, as any practice, an ongoing process. We walk before we run, and start with a 5k before we run a marathon. When we start our practice, we need help grounding ourselves in the presence of God. This help comes both in the form of our daily life and of our prayer life. Brother Lawrence breaks down the practice of the presence of God into three stages:

1. *Practicing the presence of God by continually repeating a short prayer or prayer word.*

   Brother Lawrence acknowledges that it is difficult at first to stay in the presence of God, since we are not used to it. He advises the use of a short prayer when our mind strays, to help us remember God always. He explains that it is not helpful to "use multiplicity of words in prayer, [since] many words and long discourses being often the occasions of wandering."[7] Brother Lawrence tells us not to be upset if our mind wanders, rather to bring it back quietly to our short prayer, and so remind ourselves of the presence of God.

   Most of the Breath Prayers in this book are short

word prayers that are repeated in the rhythm of our breath. They are simple, easy to remember and helpful on our long journey from "the mind into the heart" as so many people call our journey with God.

2. *Practicing the presence of God by staying in the present moment, being attentive in all we do.*

This step might be slightly more difficult, because we are not used to praying this way. It is mainly a shift in our perception of prayer. I think it is one of the most simple, and at the same time difficult, things for us adults to do — to stay in the present moment. Small children know how to do it, but adults are trained to multitask.

Brother Lawrence asks us to stay in the moment and put "simple attention" into all we do. I know that it does not feel like prayer to most of us to wash the dishes, make the beds or attend to whatever small tasks we have to do during the day. It is the "simple attention," though, that will take us out of our mind and to the part of our being that connects with God. It is not about changing what we do, but changing with how much love and gratitude we do it. If we live a moral life, put our attention into our tasks, and know that God is always with us, our life becomes a prayer to God.

This attentiveness in the present moment is also important when we ask God for help. We often pray to God in preparation for a given event, but then forget to be aware of God as the event unfolds. Even our prayers of petition need to happen in the presence of God in the present moment.

The Prayers of Presence are created in a way that they are an anchor and a reminder during specific daily tasks. You will be reminded of the presence of God when you take a shower, switch on the light, stand in line at the grocery store, brush your teeth and more tasks. The prayers are designed in a simple way to help you connect with God in all that you do.

3. *Practicing the presence of God by being present with God in your soul.*

We now come to the part of Brother Lawrence's teachings that cannot be conveyed with words. It is what other spiritual teachers, such as St. Benedict, Thomas Merton, Thomas Keating and Macrina Wiederkehr, have called contemplation, or communion with God. Macrina Wiederkehr describes it this way: "My contemplation I cannot show you, nor should I. If my contemplation, if my deep being in God, is healthy, it will show up in the way I live my daily life. You will see the results of that contemplation in my life lived out."[8] In the book *The Cloud of Unknowing,* the anonymous author writes, "I am at a loss to say more, for the experience is beyond words."[19]

Embracing "Him with a tenderness that cannot be expressed, and which experience alone can teach us to understand,"[20] is the state that Brother Lawrence refers to as "actual union" or "perfect union."[21] This stage is beyond communication and, by the grace of God, we too will experience it one day. It can happen at any moment in our lives and does not depend on what we do, or how long we have practiced the presence of God, because "He will come in His own time, and when you least expect it."[22] Brother Lawrence's faith in God was so strong that he was not afraid, even when German soldiers thought he was a spy and threatened to hang him. He told them calmly that he was not guilty of any crime but he was quite ready to die and be with God. The soldiers released him!

PRAYING PAUSE

What would it feel like to be this close to God? Do you want to be this close or would it be frightening?... How would your life change if you were able to receive God's guidance continually?...

Take a few minutes to ponder these questions. If you are a person who likes to write, meditate on paper and see where it leads you.

Let's summarize Brother Lawrence's spiritual teachings into the most important points:

~ God lives within our soul and is closer than we know.

~ We cannot know God by understanding, but by faith and love alone.

~ To know God, we have to know ourselves.

~ We have to let go of mistakes in the past and immediately ask God's forgiveness when we make mistakes, then let them go and not dwell on them.

~ This way of praying is difficult at first, but if we persevere, it will bring us into deep joy and peace.

~ We learn to pray this way by getting out of our head and into our heart. Using short prayers will help us as well as doing everything with "simple attention."

~ We will by the grace of God experience union with God one day and it doesn't matter where we are in our spiritual journey. It happens by God's grace.

Though the theology behind the Prayers of Presence is Brother Lawrence's, Anthony De Mello provides a beautiful metaphor for the above truth:

"Is there anything I can do to make myself Enlightened?"

"As little as you can do to make the sun rise in the morning."

"Then of what use are the spiritual exercises you prescribe?"

"To make sure you are not asleep when the sun begins to rise."[23]

The Physical and Neurological Effect of the Prayers of Presence

*Not only do prayer and spiritual practice
reduce stress and anxiety, but just twelve minutes of
meditation per day may slow down the aging process.*
—Andrew Newberg and Mark Robert Waldman

Since I was a little girl I have been fascinated by the fact that we think. I remember asking myself when I was about five years old whether I could stop thinking.

I sat in the courtyard with my grandmother in silence, both of us listening to the birds. When I got bored, I wondered where my thoughts came from and tried not to think. At one point I thought I had succeeded and thought, "Oh, I am not thinking" and realized that I had just thought again. The fascination of the process of thinking and how we get to certain topics in the process has not left me. I have traced a train of thought back to its beginning many times in my life. I have also been fascinated by the question of whether our thoughts influence our emotions or the other way around. What makes us think positive thoughts and what triggers negative ones? Can we change the way we think?

In this chapter I will explain how the Prayers of Presence help you change the habit of negative thinking into a positive connection with life and God. I will also explain how practicing the Prayers of Presence will affect your physical well-being by reducing the stress level in your life. My main sources are the books *My Stroke of Insight* by Jill Bolte Taylor and *How God Changes Your Brain* by Andrew Newberg and Mark Robert Waldman. I found many of my questions answered in these wonderful books.

Jill Bolte Taylor, a Harvard neurologist, experienced a stroke in the left hemisphere of her brain in 1996. As a neurologist, she became aware of what was happening to her and while she was having the stroke, she thought, "Wow, this is so cool! Wow, how many scientists have the opportunity to study their own brain function and mental deterioration from the inside out?"[1]

In her humorous and intelligent voice, Dr. Taylor describes what happened when she lost the function of her left-brain hemisphere and experienced the world from the right-brain hemisphere. She writes: "As the language centers in my left hemisphere grew increasingly silent and I became detached from the memories of my life, I was comforted by an expanding sense of grace. In this void of higher cognition and details pertaining to my normal life, my consciousness soared into an all-knowingness, a 'being at one' with the universe, if you will. I no longer perceived myself as a whole object separate from everything."² She goes on to describe the progress of her stroke and her inability to function normally. As her left side deteriorated, she experienced peace, and the little voices that "kept me abreast of myself in relation to the world outside of me, were delightfully silent. And in their absence, my memories of the past and the future evaporated. I welcomed the reprieve that the silence brought from the constant chatter that related me to what I now perceived as the insignificant affairs of society... For the first time, I felt truly at one with my body as a complex construction of living, thriving organisms."³ I am sure that none of us wants to experience a stroke and have to go through what Dr. Taylor did, but wouldn't it be wonderful to experience the peace she describes as we tend to the day-to-day affairs of our life? The Prayers of Presence help you shift your awareness to the right side of your brain without having to experience a stroke. You will find the peace Dr. Taylor writes about simply by practicing these prayers every day.

Dr. Taylor explains in a rudimentary way how the two hemispheres of our brain work together. While the right hemisphere takes life in moment by moment and "creates a master collage of what this moment in time looks like, sounds like, tastes like, smells like and feels like,"⁴ the left hemisphere takes "...each of those rich and complex moments created by the right hemisphere and strings them together in a timely succession. By organizing details in a linear and methodical configuration, our left brain manifests the concept of time whereby our moments are divided into the past, present and future."[5] When we look back to Brother Lawrence's way of practicing the presence of God, it seems to me that he must have switched his awareness from the left side of the brain to the right simply by being aware of God in all he did. Brother Lawrence and many other spiritual teachers confirm that we can only experience God in the present moment, and for the right-brain hemisphere "no time exists other than the present moment, and each moment is vibrant with sensation. The experience of joy happens in the present moment."[6]

PRAYING PAUSE

Rest in your breathing and become aware of your surroundings. What do you hear?... What do you see?... By becoming aware of your surroundings, you just shifted your awareness into your right brain and came into the present moment... Do you feel more peaceful as a result?

So are we able to change our negative thoughts by coming into the present moment and stop worrying, as Jesus asks us to do? "Therefore do not worry about tomorrow, for tomorrow will worry about itself. Each day has enough trouble of its own" (Matt 6:34 NIV). Dr. Taylor seems to think so: "I am in control of how I choose to think and feel about those things. Even negative events can be perceived as valuable life lessons, if I am willing to step to the right and experience the situation with compassion."[7] If we trust Dr. Taylor's experience and her professional expertise, we know that even though we are not in control of our lives, we are in control of our thoughts. "Based upon my experience with losing my left mind, I wholeheartedly believe that the feeling of deep inner peace is neurological circuitry located in our right brain. This circuitry is constantly running and always available for us to hook into. The feeling of deep inner peace is something that happens in the present moment. It's not something that we bring with us from the past or project into the future. Step one to experiencing inner peace is the willingness to be present in the right here, right now."[8]

In my work as a spiritual director, I like to use the metaphor of a lake to describe the different sides of our brain. In the following meditation the left brain symbolizes the surface of the lake and the right brain symbolizes the depth of the lake.

PRAYING PAUSE

Read this meditation slowly and then visualize the following image for a few moments... Rest in your

*breathing and relax your jaw, your shoulders and
your stomach... Now imagine yourself at the bottom
of a lake. Magically, you can breathe under water. Sit
comfortably, quietly and peacefully and feel the cool
water surround you. It is just the right temperature
and the beautiful blue soothes your soul. Look up
and see the surface above you. The surface of the lake
constantly changes: Sometimes it is windy and the
surface has soft ripples and at other times it is
stormy and has big waves with whitecaps built up.
Sometimes it is calm and quiet and the surface is
smooth like glass and at other times it is raining and
the raindrops form little craters on the lake.
Sometimes it is hot and the sun scorches the lake's
surface and other times it is cold and the surface of
the lake is frozen. You are comfortably and quietly
sitting at the depth of the lake, watching and
enjoying all the changes. Where you are sitting, it is
always calm. It is always quiet. It is always a
comfortable temperature. It is always the same quiet
movement. It is always the same consistency. You
feel like the psalmist who writes:*

*Surely I have calmed and quieted my soul, Like a
weaned child with his mother; Like a weaned
child is my soul within me.*—Psalm 131:3(KJV)

We have a choice to either live on the surface of the

lake, which represents the mind (left brain), or at the depth of the lake, which represents the heart and our union with God (right brain).

So how do we tap into this circuitry of the right side of our brain? There are many possibilities that Dr. Taylor shares with us in the chapter "Finding Your Deep Inner Peace."[9] Whether you ask yourself what it feels like to be "you" (Body Awareness Prayer "Feeling") at any given moment, observe your breathing (Breath Prayer "Breathing in God Deeply"), consciously taste your food (Daily Awareness Prayer "Eating") or listen to music (Body Awareness Prayer "Listening"), the key to finding peace is to slow down your mind and "come back to the here and now."[10]

If that is how we find peace from a scientific point of view, why not add the dimension of our faith and make it into a prayerful experience? Andrew Newberg and Mark Robert Waldman found that "if you incorporate your ethical, spiritual, or religious beliefs into these exercises, they can become even more meaningful and experientially rich."[11] What happens in our bodies when we come into the present moment and shift our awareness into the right hemisphere of our brain with meditation and prayer? Through brain scans, Newberg and Waldman found that "meditation teaches you how to alter the functioning of each of these parts of the brain in ways that improve your physical and emotional health. Indeed, it can even change the way your brain perceives reality."[12] Wow!

The following explanations of how contemplative prayer and meditation change our brain are mostly taken from *How God Changes Your Brain*. The authors, Newberg and Waldman, and their research staff at the University of Pennsylvania and the Center for Spirituality and the Mind, conducted numerous studies and brain scans to find out how our brains change when we pray and meditate. One of the studies Newberg and Waldman conducted were brain scans on Franciscan nuns and Buddhist practitioners while they prayed and meditated. They watched the neurological changes in their brains and the results are fascinating. Here are some of the overall points the authors make:

~ Spiritual practices, even when stripped of religious beliefs, enhance the neural functioning of the brain in ways that improve physical and emotional health.

~ Intense, long-term contemplation of God and other spiritual values appear to permanently change the structure of those parts of the brain that control our moods, lead to our conscious notions of self, and shape our sensory perceptions of the world.

~ Contemplative practices strengthen a specific neurological circuit that generates peacefulness, social awareness and compassion for others.[13]

The studies also show "how spiritual practices improve memory, and how they can slow down neurological damage caused by growing old."[14] The research with memory patients suggests "that meditation can help maintain a healthy structural balance that will slow the aging process."[15]

PRAYING PAUSE

Take a break and come into the present moment of your breath... How are you doing right now?... This tiny shift, becoming aware of the present moment, will bring you closer to yourself and God.

In chapter eight, "Exercising Your Brain," the authors describe the results of their research on the eight best ways to enhance our physical, mental and spiritual health.[16] They ranked all suggestions in terms of the most effective way to enhance our health and came to the conclusion that the number one best way is faith.[17] Brother Lawrence knew by faith what we now learn by scientific methods and research.

Faith plays an important role in all we do in the world because we can't be "...a hundred percent sure about anything. We can't even trust our eyes when it comes to something as obvious as color, because color doesn't exist in the world. Light waves exist, but we can't see them at all... The same can be said about God. We can take surveys, or scan people's brains as they contemplate God, but this will tell us more about the brain and nothing about the true nature of the universe."[8] Having faith and believing in God changes our brain in positive ways and if we meditate or pray contemplatively, "...we improve our physical, emotional, and cognitive health, adding years of greater happiness to our lives... They will boost the responsiveness of your immune system, sharpen your productivity at work, and enrich the quality of your relationships — not just with family and friends, but with strangers whom you might casually meet. Empathy and compassion will be enhanced, and you'll even find it easier to interact with those who hold beliefs that differ from your own."[9]

If this is all true, why do so many of us have difficulties (and even resistance to) establishing a contemplative prayer practice? Newberg and Waldman have an answer for us: "After spending decades building a somewhat stable personality to handle life's tribulations, the brain is hesitant to alter its underlying beliefs. After all, even if your behavior is dysfunctional, it has helped you to survive, which is what your brain is primarily designed to do. It took your brain decades to

form these habits, and it's not easy to turn them off...
Furthermore, any disruption in old neural patterns
creates a certain degree of anxiety in the brain... Thus,
it's easy to dream up a new idea, but exceedingly
difficult to get the rest of the brain to comply. Even if
you succeed in changing different aspects of your
personality, don't be surprised if old patterns of
behavior reassert themselves from time to time."[20]

I have explained it to one of my spiritual directees
this way:

*Imagine your brain as a big thick forest with lots of
undergrowth, trees, bushes and other plants. You
have cleared paths through all those years of your
life by repeating old patterns again and again. The
paths are wide and easy to walk on. If you come to
a situation in your life where you want to change a
pattern, let's say start a contemplative prayer
practice, you have to clear a new path in your
brain. Your intention is good and you clear away
the brush by starting to pray contemplatively and
you feel good about yourself. The next days you
clear away more brush, but it is getting harder and
darker the further you go into the bush. It is also
scary because there is no path to follow and it is
unknown at this point whether you will like what
you get into. Then something happens in your life –
for instance, a friend comes to visit at the time you*

were going to pray, so you don't pray; after all, it would be rude to let your friend wait. So a few days go by and you forget to pray; you return to the easy wide path you have always walked on. The new path slowly grows back over. When you remember to pray again, the path has grown over a bit and you have to clear it again. It clears more easily now because you have already worked on it.

No wonder it is so difficult to establish a new prayer practice! And because it upsets our brain and causes anxiety in our life, it is so much easier just to stick to the same old routine we are used to. So how do we make this change happen? Newberg and Waldman suggest we do three ". . . things: a conscious commitment to make a small improvement every day, a good dose of social support to help you honor that commitment, and a hefty serving of optimism and faith."[21] I would add, a willingness to practice the Prayers of Presence every day.

I am sure your intention is to be closer to God in life because you are reading this book. Practicing God's presence is a process and the first step is to know why you want to be closer to God. Newberg and Waldman found that, "When you clearly articulate your intention or goal in writing or speech, your frontal lobes can more efficiently direct your motor cortex to carry out your desire as you actively engage with others in the world.

It's an extraordinary process: You begin with a goal-oriented thought, and the more you focus on it, the more your brain begins to plot out strategies to carry out that thought into the world."[22]

Praying Pause

If you are a person who likes to write, meditate on the following question that way; otherwise, take a few minutes and ponder the question and share it with somebody: Why do you want to feel closer to God?

THE PSYCHOLOGICAL AND EMOTIONAL EFFECT OF THE PRAYERS OF PRESENCE

But when we lift our cup to life, we must dare to say:
'I am grateful to all that has happened to me
and led me to this moment.'
—Henri Nouwen (1932-1996)

The act of praying is powerful. We've looked at the positive neurological and physical effect of prayers, but they are beneficial in other ways too. This chapter explores their psychological and emotional effect on us, and addresses the following questions: *How do we pray? To whom do we pray? How do the Prayers of Presence affect our lives?*

How Do We Pray?

When we hear the word "pray," we all have our own understanding of what it means. We have been molded by various experiences; each of us has different images of God and who God is in our lives. These experiences influence how we pray and how much faith we have that our prayers are heard.

Most scholars agree that the Bible was written in Greek, and the Greek word for pray "proseúxomai" translates into: "pray – literally, to interact with the Lord by switching human wishes (ideas) for His wishes as He imparts faith ("divine persuasion")."[1] Richard Rohr, a contemporary Franciscan monk, says it beautifully: "Prayer is not about changing God, but being willing to let God change us."[2]

Prayer is often experienced as talking to God. But even though we talk to God, we rarely make space for listening. We might add, "Thy will be done," but really hope that "Thy will" is according to "my will." Rohr defines prayer as "any interior journeys or practices that allow you to experience faith, hope, and love within yourself. It is not a technique for getting things, a pious exercise that somehow makes God happy, or a requirement for entry into heaven. It is much more like practicing heaven now."[3] Frederick Buechner, a Presbyterian minister and writer, describes prayer "...not as speaking to God, which in a scattered way I do many times a day because I cannot help doing it, but prayer as being deeply silent, as watching and listening for God to speak."[4] Brother Lawrence "often spent the entire time of prayer set aside in the monastic day in rejecting thoughts and falling back into them."[5] Brother Lawrence was in fact practicing what we call Centering Prayer today.

I like to think of prayer as connecting my life into the life of God. Prayer means many different things to people and the most important thing is to find out what it means to each one of us.

PRAYING PAUSE

Become aware of the rhythm of your breathing...
Before you read on, take a few minutes to
meditate on the following questions: Why do you
pray? How do you pray?

The Prayers of Presence are part of the Contemplative tradition of Christianity. The word "contemplation" comes from the Latin root "cum" (with, together), "temp" (making a notch), and "lation" (repeated action). Culturally, we often use the word "contemplating" as thinking and ruminating about things, but that is not the meaning of contemplation in the Christian tradition. In Contemplation, we actually go beyond our thoughts and shift our awareness into our hearts "...believing that in truth God is in our hearts,"[6] as Brother Lawrence so beautifully said. Father Thomas Keating, a Trappist monk and one of the fathers of the contemporary movement of Centering Prayer, writes that "Contemplative Prayer is the world in which God can do anything, in which the inspiration of the Spirit is given directly to our spirit without the intermediary of our own reflections or acts of will. In other words, the Spirit prays in us and we consent. Contemplative Prayer is not so much the absence of thoughts as detachment from them. It is the opening of mind and heart, body and emotions – our whole being – to God, the Ultimate Mystery, beyond words, thoughts and emotions – beyond, in other words, the psychological content of the present moment."[7] If we use the words of neurologist Dr. Jill Bolte Taylor, contemplative prayer means that we switch our awareness from the left-brain hemisphere to the right, where "no time exists other than the present moment, and each moment is vibrant with sensation."[8] Whatever language we use – scientific, religious or psychological – let's not be overly concerned with the words we are using because they all convey the same message: We need to live in the present moment because God is in *every* moment!

Most of us do not know how to do this. We have become used to a compartmentalized life: this is work, this is free time, this is time with my husband and children, this is housework and this is prayer time. We perceive some of our time as fun but most of our time as work, including our jobs, errands and chores. How many of us work in order to be able to pay the rent and groceries and not because we enjoy what we do? An attitude many of us have adopted is that we "need to get things done" to be able to enjoy life in the future or we just have "to get through this" and then we will live a happy life.

I was certainly guilty of living this way before I had an epiphany a few summers ago. I was jolted into the present moment by the beauty of nature and finally understood what it meant to enjoy every moment in life. I was on my last days of vacation at our cottage in Canada when I discovered that I needed to repair the boathouse roof. I had been looking forward to enjoying my last days canoeing on the lake, relaxing, and having fun before I had to go back to my busy life in Florida. I certainly did not want to spend my last days working, but the repair needed to be done before the winter. On this particular morning, I got hammer, nails and shingles and went up on the roof. I was resentful and wanted to get it over with as quickly as possible. I don't remember what made me look up from my work, but I was stunned by the beauty I saw. The lake glistened in the sun and a beautiful cool breeze made the water look like a million diamonds were dancing on it. Time stood still!

I realized that it did not matter whether I was canoeing or repairing the roof; I was still on the lake, enjoying the beauty of it, getting exercise and experiencing God's presence in my life. I was grateful beyond measure for this moment of clarity and conversion. I realized by the grace of God that I had created my own divided reality and I suddenly had "eyes to see" (Mark 8:18 NIV), thereby experiencing what Brother Lawrence had said so many years ago: "He will come in His own time, and when you least expect it."⁹ I certainly did not expect God on the boathouse roof. I was jolted into the presence of God by the beauty I saw when I looked up. The lake had always been there, the sun had been shining for hours and the breeze had been blowing for a while. It had all been there, but I had been too wrapped up in negative thoughts and feelings. God was present and I was absent!

Margaret Guenther, a spiritual director and former director of the Center for Christian Spirituality at General Theological Seminary in New York, writes, "We hear God speak, predictably in sacred settings, but also in wildly unlikely places and circumstances: the subway, the shower and the messy garage. After all, the Holy Spirit is blowing over us all the time... It is all a matter of paying attention."¹⁰ The Holy Spirit literally blew over me, and repairing the boathouse roof became a prayer. When we live in the presence of God, we do not need to divide our life into "work and play" or "good and bad." Our life is our life no matter what happens. We will be able to accept every facet of our lives as meaningful and as an opportunity to grow.

To Whom Do We Pray?

PRAYING PAUSE

> *Rest in your breathing for a moment... Become aware of your surroundings and gently meditate on the following quote: "Your image of God creates you — or defeats you. There is an absolute connection between how you see God and how you see yourself and the whole universe."*
> *—Richard Rohr*

One of the most important questions in prayer is "To whom do we pray?" Before I go into more details about the psychological influence of the Prayers of Presence, I want to look at this question very carefully because it has an enormous effect on our emotional health. We can pray the most loving, heartfelt prayers, but if we pray to a God who is angry, vengeful, judgmental and unforgiving, we will most likely not have our prayers answered because we don't expect them to be. If we experience God this way, it can damage our brain.[11] But praying to "...a loving God rather than a punitive God reduces anxiety, depression, and stress and increases feelings of security, compassion and love."[12]

PRAYING PAUSE

Breathe naturally and become aware of your thoughts and feelings... To whom do you pray?... Use your breath to stay in the present moment when your thoughts take you into the past or the future...

Whether we are conscious of it or not, we all have an image of God. According to Newberg and Waldman, "From a neurological perspective, images of God are unavoidable."[3] We have to accept that our brain works this way or we might damage our relationship with God by staying stuck in our childhood image.[4] Newberg and Waldman conducted several studies of people's images of God. They created an online questionnaire with over 1,000 participants to find out how people perceive God and what God means to them. They summarize results that indicate most perceive "...a God that maintains its mystery, a very intimate experience that cannot be captured by words."[5] When asked what God felt like, most people answered "God felt like love!"[6] Brother Lawrence told us that, "...if the will can in any measure come to know God, it can do so only through love."[7]

PRAYING PAUSE

What does God feel like to you?... Take a few moments and meditate on this question... When

*do you feel God's presence most?... What does it
feel like?...Try to go into the feeling...*

Our image of God changes throughout our lives. As
children we visualize God as a person because our brain
has not yet developed the ability to have abstract ideas.
As we go through life, our use of symbols increases, but
"when it comes to our most primal sense of God, it all
begins with a face."[8] When we mature and are able to
perceive God in more abstract ways, we can change our
image of God. If the new perceptions "...are repeated,
old memory circuits can be permanently changed. Still,
our childhood notions of God will continue to
influence our thoughts. This too is seen in adult
pictures of God."[9]

We all know the commandment, "You shall not
make for yourself an image in the form of anything in
heaven above or on the earth beneath or in the waters
below" (Exodus 20:4 NIV), but at the same time, we
find many different images for God in the Bible. God is
portrayed as king, general, judge, lover, father, mother,
fire, water, wind, shepherd, rock, a still small voice and
many other images. Margaret Guenther loves the image
of God as a rock. "When the psalmist says that God is
his rock and his stronghold, he is not saying that God is
a geological formation or a fortified building. Rather he
is offering us a picture, one picture of the essentially
unknowable God."[20] Guenther knows that God is

45

infinite, eternal, and unchanging "...and my rock is not. But that rock is a picture, an image, a metaphor that expresses my yearning for safety and a sense of God's presence. That rock tells me something about God that even the most eloquent words and compelling logic fail to do."[21]

I have different images that work for me at different times. I treasure my metaphor of God as the ocean. This metaphor allows me to pray with God who is bigger than I am but also within me. It replaces my old childhood picture of God that was very close to Santa Claus. I am a visual person and have different imagery that connects me with God at different times. At times I need the feeling of being wrapped into God's arms, as Psalm 131 suggests:

> *Surely I have calmed and quieted my soul,*
> *Like a weaned child with his mother;*
> *Like a weaned child is my soul within me.*
> —Psalm 131:3 (KJV)

At other times I listen to God's "still, small voice" (1 Kings 19:12 KJV) in Centering Prayer and am spiritually nourished by a God whose "first language is silence."[22]

Jesus often referred to God as "Father." He freed us from the punishing, judgmental and vengeful God of the Old Testament and made it possible for us to have a personal relationship with God. Thomas Hart, a therapist and spiritual director who taught theology at Seattle University, writes, "...blockages to human growth can be cleared when people are helped to revise their images of God."[23]

I can relate to this well. My image of God as father kept me from trusting God for a long time. I grew up with an alcoholic and emotionally abusive father whose authority was unpredictable. I have a very different relationship with God now, but I believe that the relationship is still affected by my male childhood image of God and my experience of my father, whom I love deeply despite his problems. Sometimes we have to deliberately choose another image of God and refuse to use the noun "He" to heal a potentially harmful image of God. I needed to get away from viewing God as male and using "Thou" and "Thee" works much better for me. It expresses the mystery of God and the awe I have for this mystery.

PRAYING PAUSE

Even though you might want to read on, take this praying pause and rest in your breathing for a moment... Do you remember images of God you had in your life?

It is safe to say that none of us knows God. God is a mystery and we all have a different relationship with this mystery. At the same time, we all have a God image in our minds, one that might not always be conscious. At a certain point in our spiritual journey, we have to examine this image to grow spiritually and as human beings.

One result of dividing our lives into sections is that some of us have cut God out of our lives and put God into church. We have also projected God into heaven, far removed from our lives. But God is in heaven and God is on earth. God is concerned with the big things in life and the small things in life. God is always with us and closer to us than our own breath. God is deep within our souls, and we can get to know God more deeply by consciously living with God in our daily lives.

How Do the Prayers of Presence Affect Our Lives?

Practicing the Prayers of Presence integrates God into every moment of our lives. It teaches us to see, feel, taste and hear God in the present moment. So often we get carried away by our hopes and fears for the future. We might not be content in our present life situation and hope for better times in the future; or, if we are happy, we might fear what the future will bring. In both scenarios, our thoughts and emotions are focused on the future and not on the present moment. According to Frederick Buechner, "What deadens us most to God's presence within us, I think, is the inner dialogue that we are continuously engaged in with ourselves, the endless chatter of human thought."[24]

Let me share an example in my life of how my inner dialogue took me away from the present moment which I only noticed in retrospect.

I was sitting in my favorite prayer chair, ready to do my morning devotion. The Bible was in my hands and a cup of green tea was steaming next to me. I was centered and enjoying the moment when suddenly my eye caught a speck of dirt on the floor. I thought, "I must have missed this spot when I vacuumed yesterday," a neutral thought in the present moment. This thought had engaged the left side of my brain and connected this moment with moments of my past. I remembered my father's voice ridiculing that I couldn't even clean well. This thought led me into a shameful memory of cleaning the living room as a 12-year-old girl. I had missed some dust balls next to the fireplace and my father pointed this out in front of all the relatives who were visiting on this particular Saturday afternoon. The old feelings of shame, inadequacy and low self-esteem caught up with me at the moment I wanted to pray, and I felt unworthy of prayer. "How can I pray, if I can't even clean right? How can God love me if my father, who knew me well, did not love me? How can God love me if I am not lovable?"

All this was going on unnoticed and I got up to get

away from these painful feelings. I suddenly felt empty and ate some chocolate to stuff the feelings down. How did I get from my intention to pray to eating chocolate? Seeing the speck of dirt triggered old memories and instead of staying in the present moment with God, I followed my thoughts down the road of painful memories. I shifted my awareness into the left-brain hemisphere and abandoned the peace I was feeling when I was grounded in my right-brain hemisphere, which only perceives the present moment. The whole process probably took less than ten seconds but instead of spending time with God in prayer, I got up and ate chocolate.

Whether we are conscious of it or not, we all have memories that interfere with our relationship with God and a blissful life. The Prayers of Presence help us heal these memories by connecting us with the present moment again and again. When we practice staying in the present moment on a regular basis, it becomes much easier to catch ourselves at other times during the day when our mind wanders from the present moment. Being present in the moment, we will notice the speck of dirt and it will be just that: a speck of dirt that we missed. Now we have the choice to vacuum it up the next time we clean or pick it up and continue with prayer. No matter what our decision, we will follow our intention of being with God in prayer. Father Thomas

Keating, a Trappist monk, calls this process "divine therapy" and God the "divine therapist."

P<small>RAYING</small> P<small>AUSE</small>

How are you feeling right now?... Becoming aware of your feelings brings you back into the present moment. Breathe gently, soften your face, relax your shoulders and sink into the chair... You are present in the here and now... Enjoy the moment.

Let me give you an example of how four specific Prayers of Presence work emotionally and how they can help heal feelings of low self-esteem, anxiety, fear of the dark and also help you with your weight.

The Prayer of Presence "Breathing in God's Love" is a breath prayer and connects you with your breath and the love of God. You say and hear "I love you" inwardly in the rhythm of your breathing. If you replace every negative thought you have about yourself with "I love you," you will soon love yourself God's way. Through practicing this prayer, I discovered that my father loved me as well as he could in his brokenness. He could not love me unconditionally because of his own issues, but it didn't mean that I was not lovable. Practicing this prayer for a few years now has changed my relationship with others. The prayer opened me up to God's love, and with God's love and light, darkness cannot prevail.

When I am worried about different topics, like my

professional career or other worries, I shift my thoughts to "Be still and know that I am God" (Psalm 46:10 NIV) and say this prayer in the rhythm of my breath to replace all other thoughts. It immediately calms me because I know it is God's truth and I have nothing to worry about. It also brings me back into the present. As Dr. Jill Bolte Taylor writes, the "feeling of deep inner peace is something that happens in the present moment. It's not something that we bring with us from the past or project into the future. Step one to experiencing inner peace is the willingness to be present in the right here, right now."[25] This prayer can help you heal anxiety and fear of the future.

The Daily Awareness Prayer "Turning on the Light" connects you with the present moment when you switch on the light by saying, "I am the light of the world." After you have prayed this prayer for a few weeks, you will notice more confidence in yourself because the repetition of this truth will have a positive effect on your self-esteem. You will become aware of God's image of you as the light of the world. A friend of mine who practiced this prayer often lost her deep-seated fear of the dark because she started believing that the light was within her. She is now able to sleep in the dark for the first time in her life.

The Prayer "Eating" guides you into the present moment while you eat. You will automatically slow your eating down and see, smell and taste the food on your plate. Unconscious feelings — such as not having enough or stuffing down negative emotions — will not be possible, because you will be aware of every bite you eat. Your body, mind and soul will appreciate the food God has provided for you. This will lead to eating more consciously and eventually eating just the right amount of food. Becoming aware of the presence of God is the best diet there is!

When we live with awareness, we interrupt negative thought patterns and can be more loving and compassionate with ourselves and others. Then we are able to follow Jesus' commandment "Love your neighbor as yourself" (Mark 12:31 NIV). When we stay in the presence of God, we know that our needs, wants and fears are fleeting and ever-changing states. Life situations come and go, just as our breath goes in and out, but our life in God never changes. We are magnificent children of God, loved unconditionally.

PRAYING PAUSE

Take a moment to read the following prayer slowly:

> *God, grant me the serenity*
> *to accept the things I cannot change,*
> *Courage to change the things I can,*
> *And the wisdom to know the difference.*
> *Living one day at a time;*

Enjoying one moment at a time;
Accepting hardship as the pathway to peace;
Taking, as He did, this sinful world
as it is, not as I would have it.
Trusting that He will make all things right
if I surrender to His Will;
That I may be reasonably happy in this life,
and supremely happy with Him
Forever in the next.
Amen.

—Reinhold Niebuhr (1892-1971)

By practicing God's presence in our daily lives, we don't have to ask how to "make time for God." God's time is our time and our time is God's time. John O'Donohue, an Irish poet and philosopher, shares a story that illustrates the beauty of living in the present moment. "My father used to tell another such story about a monk named Phoenix who was reading his breviary in the monastery. A bird began to sing, and the monk listened so purely to the song of the bird that he was aware of nothing else. Then the song stopped, and he took up his breviary and went back into the monastery to discover that he no longer recognized anyone there. And they did not recognize him either. He named all his fellow monks with whom he had lived up to what seemed half an hour before, but they had all disappeared. The new monks looked up their annals, and sure enough, years and years before, a monk Phoenix had mysteriously disappeared. At the metaphorical level, this story claims that through real presence the monk Phoenix had actually broken into eternal time. There is an eternal region within us where we are not vulnerable to the ravages of normal time."[26] May we all learn to live in eternal time!

PRACTICING THE PRAYERS OF PRESENCE

Rejoice always, pray without ceasing,
in everything give thanks,
for this is the will of God in Christ Jesus for you.
—1 Thessalonians 5:16-17 (NKJV)

P RAYING PAUSE
Pray and meditate on Psalm 139:1-18 (NIV) for a
while and let the words live in you:

> *You have searched me, Lord,*
> *and you know me.*
> *You know when I sit and when I rise;*
> *you perceive my thoughts from afar.*
> *You discern my going out and my lying down;*
> *you are familiar with all my ways.*
> *Before a word is on my tongue*
> *you, Lord, know it completely.*
> *You hem me in behind and before,*
> *and you lay your hand upon me.*
> *Such knowledge is too wonderful for me,*
> *too lofty for me to attain.*
> *Where can I go from your Spirit?*
> *Where can I flee from your presence?*
>
> *If I go up to the heavens, you are there;*

if I make my bed in the depths, you are there.
If I rise on the wings of the dawn,
*   if I settle on the far side of the sea,*
*   even there your hand will guide me,*
*   your right hand will hold me fast.*
If I say, "Surely the darkness will hide me
*   and the light become night around me,"*
*   even the darkness will not be dark to you;*
*   the night will shine like the day,*
*   for darkness is as light to you.*
For you created my inmost being;
*   you knit me together in my mother's womb.*
I praise you because I am fearfully and
*   wonderfully made;*
*   your works are wonderful,*
*   I know that full well.*
My frame was not hidden from you
*   when I was made in the secret place,*
*   when I was woven together in the depths of*
*   the earth.*
Your eyes saw my unformed body;
*   all the days ordained for me were written in*
*   your book*
*   before one of them came to be.*
How precious to me are your thoughts, God!
How vast is the sum of them!
Were I to count them,

they would outnumber the grains of sand—
when I awake, I am still with you.

Practicing the presence of God the way Brother Lawrence did by praying without ceasing seems daunting and almost impossible in our everyday lives. With our lives so full, many of us can't even find the time to pray much less meditate several times a day. How can we pray without ceasing? How can we live in the presence of God and make God our focus in life? How can we make our life a prayer?

The real question is, how can we *not* make God the focus of our lives? If we believe that God lives within us and we live within God, then self-will cuts us off from the divine. When we pray the Prayers of Presence, we say yes to God's life within us and acknowledge that we are part of something bigger than ourselves. We are:

~ *Allowing God to live through us,*

~ *Accepting ourselves and our lives exactly as they are and*

~ *Acting with awareness of God's presence within us.*

The first two attitudes of *allowing* and *accepting* are internal and require more of an unlearning and surrendering, while the third suggestion of *acting* requires a change in how we do things.

Living life in a mindset of *allowing, accepting* and *acting* leads us into a spiritual adventure and a life filled with God's love, joy and peace. We learn to open our hearts to God's will and we embark on a God-conscious adventure. If we *allow* God to work through us, it will deepen our *acceptance* of ourselves and our lives, which will deepen our prayer life, which will *allow* God to work more deeply through us, which will deepen our *acceptance* of ourselves and our lives even more. It is a self-perpetuating spiral that takes us continuously deeper into our relationship with God. The good news is that we cannot make a single mistake in this process. Anita Moorjani describes our journey into God consciousness as "...a kaleidoscope that turns from one exquisite image into the next, perfection is constantly in motion. To me, this means seeing beauty in the journey and in the apparent mistakes as they take me to another level of understanding."[1]

Allowing God to Live Through Us

PRAYING PAUSE

> *Then the Lord God formed man from the dust of the ground, and breathed into his nostrils the breath of life; and the man became a living being.*—Genesis 2:7 (NRSV)

Rest in God's breath of life for a moment...
Observe your breathing... Trust God's breathing
within you... Surrender... Did you notice how
difficult it is to let your breathing flow naturally
once you have noticed it? I always try to control
my breath once I am aware of it. I usually breathe
more deeply because I know that it is good for
me... Try it again... Rest in your breathing without
changing it... Let God's breath and life flow
through you...

Our breath is a metaphor for God's guidance in our lives. God is always leading us and we often are not aware of it. If we do become aware of it, we want to take control and change it! As spiritually aware people, we want to do everything "right" to live a godly life, hoping that if we just pray enough, exercise enough and try hard enough, life will be perfect and we will not experience challenges, illness or pain. But life has challenges, illness and pain. All we have to do is find God in them and allow God to help us through them. Often the "dark night of the soul," as John of the Cross calls these times, are the ones that bring us closer to God. David Frenette has a wonderful analogy in his book *The Path of Centering Prayer*: "Transformation is in the night. When out in the country, have you ever settled into the twilight experience? What happens to your sight? Your eyes slowly begin to adjust to the darkness. After a while, you begin to see in a new way. You begin to develop night vision. With night vision, you can see by the subtle light of the stars, a light that was always there, even during the day. During the day time, the sun overwhelms the stars, so you never know there is another light possible—until the night comes. With night, a whole new universe opens up above you, subtle, brilliant and beautiful. This new world grows as long as you let it, as long as you avoid turning on an artificial light. You receive the gift of a new kind of transforming vision in the night."[2]

The stars at night are breathtakingly beautiful; however, we often focus on artificial lights in this world. Turning our focus away from them will enable us to commune with God. We are then given the gift of experiencing the extraordinary in the ordinary, and this moves us closer to the miracle of God consciousness. Every life experience is beautiful and full of God's grace, if we accept this gift.

PRAYING PAUSE

> *"Darkness deserves gratitude. It is the alleluia*
> *point at which we learn to understand that all*
> *growth does not take place in the sunlight."*
> —Joan Chittister

> *Rest in a gentle breath and remember a time*
> *when you felt the most pain in your life... What is*

*your "dark night of the soul" experience?... How
did you grow from it?*

One of my "dark nights of the soul" was during my
upbringing in Germany after the Second World War. I
was born in 1957, twelve years after the war ended and
the Nazis were officially defeated. However, that didn't
mean the horror was over; it lived on in the people who
had experienced it. They still lived in fear and were
stunned and shocked by what had happened. The
atmosphere in post-war Germany was one of
unbelievable confusion and darkness.

I spent most of my younger years with my
grandmother, who had opposed the Hitler regime. She
didn't believe in God because she reasoned that, if there
had been a God, the Nazi Reich would not have
happened. She also despised the church because its
leaders had sided with the Nazis. My father also hated
the church because of his upbringing during the Nazi
regime, but he did believe in God. My mother, on the
other hand, loved church and had a strong faith in a
loving God, which she never lost. She prayed with me
every night and taught me the Lord's Prayer when I was
three years old. I was caught in the midst of these
different beliefs and confused, but I knew one thing for
sure: God and Jesus were real!

In the summer my grandmother and I often sat in
the courtyard of our house and she would tell me

stories about her youth, about the beauty of the simple life in the early 1900s, her time as a train conductor and other wonderful tales. In the winter, we would sit in front of her little wood stove, no lights in the room except the glow of the crackling fire. She would tell me stories and I could smell the roasting apple peel on the stove. Every time, though, the stories would end with the death of two of her beloved children. Her youngest son died at the age of 27 and her only daughter died at age 36. She would share her pain with me before falling into silence and grief. I sat with her, at times not knowing where to turn with the pain; her pain over the loss of her children, and my pain that she would never love me as much as she had loved them. However, it got less painful when I remembered my mother telling me to turn to Jesus when I needed help. So I did just that, and invited him into our pain. And Jesus came. Then Jesus, my grandmother and I sat in silence for what seemed to be hours at a time and I knew I was not alone in holding the excruciating pain of loss.

I was still a little girl though, becoming bored and antsy in my chair, but I didn't dare get up and leave my grandmother. I now see that it was the beginning of practicing the presence of God in my life. In order to not think about my dead uncle and aunt, I would practice what I now know as Centering Prayer, which took me beyond my thoughts. It gave me a deep peace and connection with God that I hadn't felt before. Because of this time, I became very comfortable with silence and sitting in silent prayer with those who might be grieving. Centering Prayer is still one of my favorite disciplines and the spiritual ground upon which my work rests. God prepared me in the darkness of this confusing time for my later work as a spiritual director. I learned how to listen deeply to others in the stillness of God's presence. The darkness during the years of my early childhood has become the light of my life and work today!

PRAYING PAUSE

> *Going a little farther, Jesus fell with his face to the ground and prayed, "My Father, if it is possible, may this cup be taken from me. Yet not as I will, but as you will."*—Matthew 26:39(NIV)

> *"Thy will be done"... Pray these four words for a moment and become aware of your resulting feelings... Can you truly surrender to God's will? Can you genuinely trust and allow God's will to be done?*

I have difficulty giving up "my will." When I am honest with myself, I have to admit that I don't always trust God. My mind says, "Yes, of course I trust God," but when I go deeper and observe what is really going on within me, I feel fear creeping up. What if God's will is not what I want? What if God's will causes pain and discomfort? Because of these unconscious fears, I hold on to my own will and cause myself the very pain and discomfort that I fear. Letting go of my own will can be incredibly difficult; however, I know I need to do so in order to let God's unconditional love flow through me and into the world. I have not trusted completely yet that the only way to find my true self, is surrendering to God. I want to trust in a power that is greater than me, a power that is all-knowing, connecting us all. God gave us free will. We can use it to control life and feel in charge or we can use it to allow God's work.

Allowing God to work through us does not mean that we don't act. It means that we surrender to God first, knowing that we don't know how God will emerge in our lives. It means praying and listening first and then allowing life and God to flow through us. The following metaphor beautifully illustrates this:

During a big flood, a man climbed on top of his house to save his life. After a while, a canoe came by and the man in the canoe offered him a ride, but the man on the roof said, "No thank you, I am waiting for God to save me and God works in mysterious ways." So the man paddled away. Then a rescue team in a rubber boat came by and they wanted to save the man. He refused to go and answered, "No thank you, I am waiting for God to save me and God works in mysterious ways." The water rose and was almost to the top of the roof when a helicopter came by and a ladder was lowered for the man to climb on. He shook his head and said, "No thank you I am waiting for God to save me and God works in mysterious ways." He finally drowned and went to heaven. He was very angry with God and asked, "Why didn't you save me? I said my prayers every night, went to church every Sunday and lived a godly life. I had faith You would save me." God looked at the man with love and said, "I first sent a canoe to save you, then a motorboat and finally I sent a helicopter."

Yes, God does work in mysterious ways; however, if we assume we know God's ways, we might miss God altogether. If we stay open to the mystery of God in the ordinary moments of life, we will encounter God's love in extraordinary ways through family, neighbors, friends and strangers.

Allowing God to work through us does require some effort on our part. We have to let go, which is often more difficult than holding on! Simply "being" and giving up control by ceasing to be in charge is difficult even though we might know that surrender is the key to a life of joy. "Surrender is perfectly compatible with taking action, initiating change, or achieving goals," writes Eckhart Tolle in his book *Practicing the Power of Now*. "But in the surrendered state a totally different energy, a different quality, flows into your doing.

Surrender reconnects you with the source-energy of Being, and if your doing is infused with Being, it becomes a joyful celebration of life energy that takes you more deeply into the Now... That's why Jesus said: 'Look at the lilies, how they grow, they neither toil nor spin.'"[3]

PRAYING PAUSE

> *Surrender your own poverty and acknowledge your nothingness to the Lord. Whether you understand it or not, God loves you, is present in you, lives in you, dwells in you, calls you, saves you and offers you an understanding and compassion which are like nothing you have ever found in a book or heard in a sermon."*
> —Thomas Merton (1915-1968)

> *This pause will take about five minutes and might be one of the most important things you do today! Take this time for yourself and if you can't do five minutes, do three minutes.*

> *Become aware of your breathing... Don't change it... If it is shallow, let it be shallow; if it is deep, let it be deep... Sit and do nothing and allow the world to go on without doing anything... Let whatever happens, happen... When your thoughts take you away from the present moment, simply come back to your breathing... Allow God's*

breathing in you and in the world... God is in charge no matter what you do... Simply sit and let everything go on around you...

The kids might be yelling, the dog might be barking, the phone might be ringing, emails might have to be answered, meetings might have to be planned... Be aware of it and simply come back to your breathing... Don't resist what is happening right now... Let life flow through you and offer no resistance to how life is right now... Surrender... God is in charge and is asking you to relax... Become aware of your breathing... Surrender to God's breathing in you... Again and again...

When you get up from this five minute break, allowing God to be in charge, you will be able to talk to the kids, attend to the dog, answer the phone, answer your emails and plan your meetings. You can do all of it in a more peaceful and gentle manner, connected to God's life within you. If you notice impatience, anger or frustration, feel it as the reality of the present moment and where you are right now in the process... Accept whatever happens in life and it will transform into God's love... Be patient with yourself... This process takes practice and patience...

Accepting Ourselves and Our Lives

One of the most difficult things in life is to accept ourselves unconditionally as we are right now. Many of us have internalized the belief that we are not good enough and that we have to change and work on ourselves to be acceptable and lovable in God's eyes. If we truly want to change, we have to accept and love ourselves the way we are. Only then will change be possible. Anthony De Mello shares a beautiful story in his book *The Song of the Bird*:

"I was a neurotic for years. I was anxious and depressed and selfish. Everyone kept telling me to change. I resented them, and I agreed with them, and I wanted to change, but simply couldn't, no matter how hard I tried. What hurt the most was that, like the others, my best friend kept insisting that I change. So I felt powerless and trapped. Then one day, he said to me, 'Don't change. I love you just the way you are.' Those words were music to my ears. Don't change. Don't change. Don't change... I love you as you are. I relaxed. I came alive. And suddenly I changed! Now I know that I couldn't really change until I found someone who would love me whether I changed or not. Is this how you love me God?"[4]

Accepting ourselves unconditionally with all our shortcomings opens us up to experience God's love. It doesn't mean that we don't need to change certain behaviors; it simply means that we are more than just the summation of our actions or habits. We are beloved children of God, made in the image of God. How can we be "bad" if we are made in God's image?

Negative behavior often comes from the illusion that we are not "good," not lovable and not one with God. Negative feelings such as fear, jealousy, competitiveness, hatred and judgment will melt away in the light of the truth of our magnificent being in God. If we realize who we are, "We will not compare ourselves with each other as if one of us were better and another worse. Each of us is an original." (Galatians 5:26 MSG). We are all unique and here to live out the glory of God, which is different for each of us. We are all part of God's puzzle and need to grow into our unique puzzle piece to create a beautiful and whole world.

PRAYING PAUSE

> *Love others as well as you love yourself.*
> —Mark 12:31 (MSG)

> *Breathe deeply and relax your jaw, shoulders, abdomen... Are you judging and criticizing yourself often? Take a moment right now and meditate on the question... Every time you become aware of judging yourself harshly, hear God say, "I love you."*

Notice how often you criticize and judge yourself throughout the day. You might judge yourself for what you do, for how you look and even how you feel... Only notice and have compassion without judging your judging... Let it flow through you and be aware... Acceptance is the key to change... You can only love others as well as you love yourself.

It is time to feel compassion and mercy for our own broken selves, our imperfect childhoods, our failures and imperfection, and accept that we are human. We have to be merciful with ourselves. "The practice of mercy opens a path of healing rooted not in violence, but in peace, love and truth," writes Wayne Mueller. "When Jesus taught his followers not to judge themselves..., he was not simply saying they should be 'nice.' He was speaking to the subtle violence we invoke in our own lives when we judge, and was also alluding to the deep healing that may arise within us when we walk a path of non-harming."[5]

PRAYING PAUSE

Sit quietly for a moment and imagine what it would be like if you accepted and loved yourself unconditionally...

Sit quietly for another moment and imagine what it would feel like if you accepted your life the way it is at this moment... Observe the feelings that come up... Only observe and be aware...

As we accept ourselves the way we are, we also have to accept our life situation the way it is at this moment. Our life situations change as the weather changes, and even though a storm doesn't last forever, we often are so preoccupied with a particular phase we're in that we don't see the big picture any more.

When we accept the impermanence of our life situations, we will be able to let go more easily and not resist the movement of life any longer. As we have so-called "bad days" and "good days," we also have joyful and painful times. When we accept every life situation as it is and stay in the present moment, we eliminate suffering because we are surrendering to life and God. That does not mean that we can't change a situation; it means that if we decide to change it, we do so according to "Thy will" with an attitude of allowing and accepting.

PRAYING PAUSE

God grant me the serenity to accept the things I cannot change, courage to change the things I can and the wisdom to know the difference.
—Reinhold Niebuhr (1892-1971)

Rest in the awareness of your breathing for a moment... Do you remember the image of the lake we talked about?... You are not just the surface of the lake with its changing ways, but you are the whole lake... Your life situation is the surface of the lake and your life is the whole lake with its much bigger undisturbed depth... Surrendering to a life situation means coming from the depth of our being that is connected with God's Being...

When we come from the depth of our soul and our connection with God, we know exactly what we need to accept and what we need to change. Changing a situation while staying grounded in God means being connected with every living being. Whatever change we make will be life-giving for all involved because it comes from love and not fear. When we are in a predicament that causes pain and anxiety, it helps to become aware of our feelings first and completely surrender and accept what is happening in the present moment. If we surrender to the situation, it doesn't mean that we are inactive and giving in. It means that we are making room for God so that we clearly will see what needs to be done and what needs to be left undone. "Surrender is needed for the divine life to come into human life,"[6] is how David Frenette expresses this truth.

One essential question we have to ask ourselves is how do we know when our decision comes from God and not our own ego? After all, God does not speak in words to most of us and often God's voice is a "still, small voice" only heard in silence. There are many examples of individuals and groups who believe that God has spoken to them and acted on it. The results were destructive rather than for the common good.

There are many ways to discern the will of God and I believe it is important to share our thoughts with other people. Church services, prayer groups, and spiritual direction groups can be helpful to give us the tools to discern God's desire for us. Others, including 12-step programs such as Alcoholics Anonymous, Al-Anon and Overeaters Anonymous, which are based on spiritual principles, can help us to find God's way in this world.

As a spiritual director, I accompany many people on their spiritual journey and can often give an objective view that is helpful. I would recommend a spiritual direction relationship to anyone, but if that is not a possibility, sharing with a trusted friend or prayer partner is always a wonderful option.

I have found one approach very helpful when I have to make a quick decision in life. I also use it for the big decisions in life. I ask myself, "Am I coming from love or am I coming from fear?"

PRAYING PAUSE

> *What a man takes in by contemplation that he pours out in love.*—Meister Eckhart (1260-1328)

*Rest in your breathing for a moment and
meditate on how you make daily decisions... Ask
yourself if you usually come from love or from
fear... Remember that God is Love...*

Acting with Awareness

I AM THE ETERNAL I AM;
I always have been, and I always will be.
In My Presence you experience Love and Light, Peace and Joy.
I am intimately involved in all your moments,
and I am training you to be aware of Me at all times.
Your assignment is to collaborate with Me
in this training process.—Sarah Young

Practicing the presence of God is only one of many ways to connect with a power greater than ourselves. To that end, it is not only important that we pray but how we pray. If we say the Lord's Prayer faithfully every night before we go to bed, but don't feel the words or are not aware of what we are saying, we are less likely to feel God's presence than if we are present with the words we pray. If we go to church every Sunday out of obligation, we are less likely to feel God's presence than if we love going to church and are present to the beauty of it. If we practice the Prayers of Presence mechanically and because it is something new to do, we are less likely to feel the presence of God than if we are open and receptive to the miracle of God in every moment of life.

If we surrender to God first, then act, we will know the right thing to do. We will know whether to change our job or change something within our job, whether to talk to the person we are not at peace with or to pray for them more deeply, whether to leave a relationship or to change something within it. Acting without awareness can do more harm than just letting things stay the way they are and praying more deeply for God's guidance and insight. When we surrender completely to God, change will occur in wonderful and miraculous ways that we could not dream of. We are not resigning ourselves to the situation but surrendering to it, which makes a big difference. Resignation is freighted with feelings of victimhood. Surrendering is letting God guide us out of the situation step by step. Surrender is a gift. It is opening our hearts to grace so that God can do for us what we cannot do for ourselves. As the Serenity Prayer quoted in the praying pause reminds us, we can only change ourselves. Acceptance of people, places and things frees us from "my will" and opens the door to "Thy will." Allowing God to work through us by accepting ourselves and our present situation requires trust and faith in God. Every time we act with awareness of God's presence within us, we grow in trust and faith.

It is easy to experience God's presence in the happy events of life but more difficult to see God's hand in the painful ones. Another step altogether is to find God in the ordinary moments of life, like brushing our teeth, making breakfast, driving the kids to school, heading to the office, answering emails, doing laundry and all the other repetitive tasks we do.

How can we learn to see the beauty and grace of God in all these things? How can we experience the extraordinary in the ordinary? How do we experience the mystery in all of life?

PRAYING PAUSE

> *There are only two ways to live your life. One is as though nothing is a miracle. The other is as though everything is a miracle.* —Albert Einstein (1879-1955)

> *Gently rest in your breathing... Take a moment and recall a typical day. How do you live each day?... Take a moment and imagine what it would be like to live every day as if it were your first day in life... Imagine what it would be like to live every day as if it were your last... Now imagine what it would be like to live every day as if it were your first and last day in life...*

If we live our lives as if everything is a miracle and completely accept who we are in the moment and act with awareness, we will feel the presence of God. We cannot control our deep experience in God by our actions, but we can make sure that we are present when God acts through us. Jesus said it this way: "So stay alert. You have no idea when he might arrive" (Matthew 25:13 MSG).

Praying with the Fruits of the Spirit

A wonderful way to stay alert and act with awareness is to pray the Prayers of Presence using the gifts we have been given by the Spirit: "But the Holy Spirit produces this kind of fruit in our lives: love, joy, peace, patience, kindness, goodness, faithfulness, gentleness, and self-control."— Galatians 5:22-23 (NTL)

Praying with love is essential to a life in God. Love is listed as the first fruit of the Spirit and the most important one. Whatever we do in life, let's do it with love as that is what we are commanded to do. Jesus said, "Love one another. As I have loved you, so you must love one another" (John 13:34 NIV). If we come into the present moment and open our hearts to whatever is in front of us and do it with love – even if it is a difficult task – we are doing God's work. If we can't do it with love, we have to ask ourselves whether we are in the right place doing the right thing.

PRAYING PAUSE

> *God doesn't look at how much we do, but with how much love we do it.*—Mother Teresa (1910-1997)

> *Allow yourself to rest in the awareness of your breathing... As Mother Teresa said, it is not about how much or how fast you read but with how much love you do it...*

Praying with joy is God's yearning for us. The second fruit of the spirit, joy, is translated as "exuberance about life" in the Bible translation *The Message*. When we were children, we knew how to live our days exuberantly, even if we grew up with hardships. Our ordinary days were full of adventure, like watching a bug, smelling a flower, running in the rain or climbing a tree. Though we looked forward to Christmas and birthdays, we still enjoyed the excitement and anticipation in the present moment.

PRAYING PAUSE

> *And he said: "Truly I tell you, unless you change and become like little children, you will never enter the kingdom of heaven."*—Matthew 18:3 (NIV)

> *What does that mean to you? Do you remember when you experienced joy as a child?... What is a*

*joyful moment for you now?... Recapture joy in
your heart and remember to live every day
joyfully.*

Praying with peace in our hearts is only possible if
we come into the present moment. Every time we
remember to come into the Now, God's peace will
deepen in us. When we worry about the future and
dwell on the pain of the past, we are not at peace. When
we come into the present moment and we discover that
we are not at peace, let's not look for it; rather, accept
how we feel in the moment and breathe in God's
presence and we will feel God's peace.

PRAYING PAUSE

*God said to Moses, "I-AM-WHO-I-AM. Tell the
People of Israel, 'I-AM sent me to you.'"*—Exodus
3:14 (MSG)

*Rest gently in your breathing and close your eyes
for a moment... How do you feel?... Accept the
feeling fully and watch it transform into peace...
Ask God's presence to envelop you and bring you
home into I AM.*

Praying with patience is important when we engage
in a new prayer routine. We have to be patient while we
practice the presence of God because it is the complete
opposite of what we have learned. We were taught to
plan for the future and to be steps ahead of what is

going on in life. It feels unsafe to be present rather than trying to control life by thinking about the future or dwelling on the past. Be patient with yourself when you begin to pray this way and you will consequently develop patience with everything else in life.

PRAYING PAUSE

> *Be still before the Lord and wait patiently for him.*—Psalm 37:7 (NIV)

> *Allow your awareness to rest in your breathing for a moment... Be patient as you watch all your feelings come up... You are allowing God to pray within you right now... Be patient with God... God is patient with you and needs your patience to pray within you.*

Praying with kindness in our hearts will allow God's kindness to work through us. Kindness and compassion are deeply intertwined. If you are compassionate in your heart, you can act with kindness toward another person no matter what they have done. Experiencing kindness is one of the most healing experiences in life.

PRAYING PAUSE

> *Three things in human life are important: the first is to be kind; the second is to be kind; and the third is to be kind.*—Henry James (1843-1916)

Be kind to yourself and relax into the moment...
Relax your jaw, your shoulders and your
abdomen... Let a feeling of kindness come up in
you...

Praying with goodness in our hearts changes the world into a better place. When we are convinced that people are inherently good and it's merely their actions that can go astray, we react in a different way. No matter what somebody has done, if we know that everyone is a child of God and good in nature, we will be able to love and forgive. We are beloved children of God no matter what we have done or left undone! When we pray with goodness in our hearts, we are affirming our own goodness and the goodness of others.

PRAYING PAUSE

God saw all that he had made, and it was very
good.—Genesis 1:31 (NIV)

Look up from this book... What do you see?...
Don't judge what you see, only look... Rest in
God's love for a moment... Feel that you are part
of God's creation and that you are "very good."

Praying with faithfulness means to make a commitment to God and prayer, even if it is difficult at times, especially when life takes over with "way more important" things. The beauty of the Prayers of

Presence is that they are part of our life and that we only have to remember to come into the present moment and the presence of God. Praying with faithfulness means to get back up when we have fallen down and recommit to the prayers with kindness, love and understanding for our frail selves. It means to pray although we might not feel like it, to pray although we might have lost faith in it, and to pray in this new way although we might be more comfortable in our old familiar ways. It means to pray because we know that God wants to pray through us.

PRAYING PAUSE

> *Don't quit in hard times; pray all the harder.*
> —Romans 12:12 (MSG)

> *Take a conscious breath and be aware of the Love that is always present, whether you feel it or not... Even if you are not full of faith, God has faith in you... Being faithful is having faith in God's faith in you.*

Praying with gentleness means to step out of the illusion that we can find God; instead, we let God find us. In the Amplified Bible translation, gentleness is translated as humility. When we pray with humility, we let go of our struggle to do everything right and give ourselves into God's gentle hands. Praying gently and with humility means to let go of feeling important or unimportant, whole or broken, better or worse and simply to be who we are: one of God's many beloved children.

PRAYING PAUSE

> *It is in deep solitude and silence that I find the gentleness with which I can truly love my brother and sister.*—Thomas Merton (1915-1968)

> *Allow your breathing to guide you into this peaceful moment... We are all beloved children of God, here on earth to live our ordinary lives in extraordinary ways with gentleness and humility. No one is special, but we are all unique...*

Praying with self-control means loving ourselves enough to pray faithfully and with discipline. Many of us have a negative emotional reaction when we hear the word *discipline*. However, it has the same Latin root as disciple and means learner. If we want to learn to be in the presence of God, we have to be a disciple and be disciplined. A spiritual discipline can also be called a spiritual ritual, which simply means that we are doing the same thing at the same time.

PRAYING PAUSE

> *Self-respect is the fruit of discipline. The sense of dignity grows with the ability to say no to oneself.*—Abraham Heschel (1907-1972)

*Allow God to be present with you through the
steady rhythm of your breathing... Observe your
in-breath and your out-breath... Your body has
natural self-control, a natural rhythm and
ritual... Self-control is inherent in you and a gift
given to you by the Spirit... Accept this gift fully.*

God has given us these "fruits" of the Spirit and, as fruits grow from a seed to a ripe fruit, so will the fruits of the Spirit ripen in us when we "water" them daily. When we practice the Prayers of Presence in the mindset of the fruits of the Spirit, we say, "YES" to God's life within us. I love how David Frenette expresses this truth: "As Christ's gentleness becomes the source of your prayer, gentleness comes through you, both in prayer and in action. In life you gradually learn to move through the busyness of our ordinary world with greater ease of Spirit."[7]

God Simply is "I AM"

PRAYING PAUSE

*The contemplative knowing of God is an
unknowing of any specific concept or thought,
because you are the one who is being known. In
contemplation, God is less an object of thought
than the subject who loves you.*—David Frenette

Become aware of your breathing... God is breathing within you... Can you feel God's presence?... Feel God's love for you without a concept of what it "should" feel like... Be open to the gift of the moment and your unique experience of God.

Brother Lawrence taught us that we have to give up the notion that we can understand God or know what God feels like. This is very difficult for us humans because we want to understand with our intellect. However, we have to allow God to make a divine presence known in a way that transcends intellectual understanding. We have to let go of our expectations of what God feels like and how God works in our lives. God's presence simply is in every ordinary moment. When you still your mind and come into the present moment, you experience "I AM." Stay open and let go of how you want to experience God so you can truly experience the living God within and all around you. We miss God if we think we know God!

PRAYING PAUSE

Understanding will never bring you Peace. That's why I have instructed you to trust in me, not in your understanding. Human beings have a voracious appetite for trying to figure things out,

r to gain a sense of mastery over their
—Sarah Young

G.. s in your very breathing right now... God is...
Feel the underlying stillness in your breath... God
simply is in your breathing... Look around you...
God simply is in what you see... Listen... God
simply is in what you hear.

The Prayers of Presence are short and simple prayers, designed to help you be aware of the presence of God in all activities of your life. They help you to live fully in the present moment and you can easily practice them throughout the day. If you spend a few minutes in the morning reading through the instructions, it will only be a matter of remembering them during the day. You might need reminders throughout the day at first, but once you have established a practice, you will automatically be reminded of the prayers in certain situations and activities. Human beings are creatures of habit and once we follow a discipline or routine, our minds and bodies remember the prayers.

I experienced this when we lived in Cambridge, Massachusetts. I walked my daughters to school when the weather was nice in the fall and spring but drove them to school in the winter. While we walked to school, we prayed at a particular street corner close to the school. When we drove to school, we often had to stop at a certain traffic light and we sang a prayer until the light turned green. When we drove to school again after having walked for months, we remembered to sing our prayer at the traffic light. It amazed me that all three of us still knew to sing our prayer at this particular traffic light.

When you pray the Prayers of Presence, you open yourself to the reality of God and realize that God has been there with you all along, even when you have not been conscious of it. "God is a continually gifting presence, an ongoing grace that you are invited to recognize in all things, at all times." David Frenette is aware of the fact that, "Often life events, even the most ordinary moments of the day, are what open you to receiving grace."[8]

The Prayers of Presence are easily integrated into daily life and you don't have to be "spiritually advanced" to practice them. All you need is your breath, your body and your daily life to practice the presence of God. You could begin your practice by choosing a prayer at the beginning of each week to focus on during that week. If you chose "Breathing in God Deeply," you could set a timer or your cell phone for a certain time or several times during the day and practice the prayer for a minute. At the beginning of the next week, you could choose another prayer and integrate it, practicing both prayers during that week. By the end of a month you would regularly pray four prayers and be aware of God's presence that much more during the day.

I would suggest that you start with a prayer that sounds inviting to you because if it feels like a chore, you might not follow through. If you discover that you don't practice every day, start fresh the next morning without judging or belittling yourself. You have to renew your commitment to God every day because there are so many things in life that ask for your attention and time. Give a little time each day to God and your life will go naturally into the direction of God. Once you have learned to see God in your daily life, you will be able to experience God in all of life.

To remember praying throughout the day, you could:

~ Set a timer.

~ Put a sticky note on your bathroom mirror and on your computer.

~ Put a reminder into your pocket, like a small cross or a precious stone.

~ Pray the gratitude prayer every time you feel lack in your life and thank God as you look upon ordinary things.

~ Pray the "I love you" prayer every time you feel unloved or have low self-esteem.

These are just a few suggestions and you will likely discover other ways to remember to pray depending on the circumstances of your life. As with everything, and particularly when we start a new routine, it is much easier when we have support from a friend or a group. Ask someone to start praying with you or start a prayer support group.

The most important thing is to just start practicing and living these prayers.

PRAYING PAUSE

> *Labor a little now, and soon you shall find great rest, in truth, eternal joy; for if you continue faithful and diligent in doing, God will undoubtedly be faithful and generous in rewarding.—Thomas a Kempis (1380-1471)*

> *Breathe gently and let this truth sink into your being...*

Having written all these words about how to practice the prayers, I encourage you to relax and not make these prayers into a "method" for accessing the presence of God. As soon as we do that, creating rules we have to follow and trying to remember all the things we have to do, we put the method between us and God. We might even judge ourselves for not doing it "right" and miss God altogether. At a certain point in our journey into God, the prayers might even cease to be a conscious effort because we will live every moment in the presence of God.

I had an eye-opening experience when I attended the ordination of one of my spiritual directees. I stayed with one of her friends who lives out in the country. I woke up early on the morning of the ordination and, while walking the beautiful grounds, I discovered a flower garden with a brick path. When I walked into the garden, I saw that the brick path was laid in the form of a spiral that led into the heart of the garden. Walking the path and praying by appreciating God's beauty in the forms of flowers, bushes, pumpkin and melon patches, I realized that the closer I came to the heart of the garden, the less I had to turn my head left and right to see all the beauty. The closer I came to the end of the spiral, the more I saw of God's beauty without having to look left, right and down to make sure I stayed on the path. When I reached the end of the spiral and arrived in the heart of the garden, I relaxed and turned around slowly to appreciate the beauty of the garden in its entirety. This walk was a beautiful metaphor for our journey into the heart of God. Practicing the Prayers of Presence, we walk right into the heart of God and, having arrived, we will not have to look "left" and "right" into the past or the future.

Brother Lawrence explains the journey this way: "Since you cannot but know that God is with you in all you undertake, that He is at the very depth and center of your soul, why should you not thus pause an instant from your outward business, and even in the act of prayer, to worship Him within your soul."⁹ Worshiping God within our soul is beyond communication and, by the grace of God, we too will experience it one day. It can happen at any moment in our lives and does not depend on what we do, or how long we have practiced the presence of God, because "He will come in His own time, and when you least expect it."¹⁰ Praying the Prayers of Presence will help us to follow Jesus' words and "Keep awake" (Mark 13:37 NRSV).

There is no right or wrong way to pray these prayers, the only "wrong" thing is not to pray at all. As Paul says, "Legalism is helpless in bringing this about; it only gets in the way. Among those who belong to Christ, everything connected with getting our own way and mindlessly responding to what everyone else calls necessities is killed off for good – crucified" (Galatians 5:23-24 MSG). We all have to find out what works best for us and our particular life situation. And as soon as we think that we have gotten it right, God might show us another way that is much better for us. When we grow spiritually, we change constantly and what is right for us today might not be right for us tomorrow.

PRAYING PAUSE

Don't take life too seriously. You'll never get out alive!—Bugs Bunny

Breathing gently, let this cartoon quote sink in and guide your way... While this point was made comically, use this prayer pause to examine the truth of life's fleeting nature. How many of our day-to-day worries will really matter in the end?

When I lived in Cambridge, Archbishop Desmond Tutu taught at the Episcopal Divinity School for a semester. At one of his lectures I attended, he said that there is only one sermon he preaches: God loves you!

Even though I have written many pages about practicing the presence of God, there is only one truth: Come into the present moment and experience God's love because in the end... *This is Living!*

PART II

THE PRAYERS OF PRESENCE

God made so many different kinds of people;
why would God allow only one way to worship?
—Martin Buber (1878-1965)

THE BREATH PRAYERS

What was delivered to Moses on tablets of stone,
as the fruits of lightning and thunder,
is now more thoroughly born in our own souls
as quietly as the breath of our own being.
—Thomas Merton (1915-1968)

As long as we are alive, we are breathing! The first thing we do when we are born is breathe in and the last thing we do when we die is breathe out. A friend of mine who was dying of cancer once shared with me her deep comfort that when she would breathe her last breath out, God would breathe her in!

The Greek word for breath is "pneuma" and can also translate to "spirit." The Hebrew word for breath is "ruah" which means "air in motion" and "spirit." When we read the word "breath" in the Bible, it also means "spirit" and vice versa, since it was one word in the original writings. It seems that people knew back then that we experience the Holy Spirit with every breath we take. In the Jewish faith, the word for God, "YHWH," was not spoken at all but breathed.[1] In the Christian tradition, the Holy Spirit as part of the Trinity was given to us through breath. "Then [Jesus] took a deep breath and breathed into them. 'Receive the Holy Spirit,' he said" (John 20:22 MSG).

PRAYING PAUSE

> *Have you ever thought about the fact that you can live weeks without food, days without water, but only minutes without breath? Close your eyes for a moment and observe your breathing...*
> *Observe the in and out movement of your breathing... Only observe.*

The average person takes about 21,600 breaths per day. If we breathe full breaths we take 4-6 breaths per minute but most of us need to take 16-20 breaths per minute. A lot of us only get 10-20% of the energy that we could get out of our breathing because we take shallow breaths.

PRAYING PAUSE

> *Pause for a moment and take a deep breath. Observe how you breathe... Does your stomach rise before your chest or does only your chest rise? Deep breathing expands our diaphragm, which means first our stomach expands and then our chest. If only your chest rises, you have only filled your upper lungs with oxygen. When you breathe in, breathe into your lower lungs so your stomach comes out first, then continue to fill*

your upper lungs so your chest rises... Breathe
this way for a few breaths... It is helpful to put the
right hand on your stomach and the left hand on
your chest to feel the movement of your
breathing... Can you feel the difference?

Isn't it amazing what we can accomplish by breathing deeply? Newberg and Waldman also found in their research that if "...you choose a phrase that has meaning for you, it will significantly enhance your practice. In fact, mere repetition of any positive phrase will reduce stress, anxiety, and anger while simultaneously improving one's quality of life."[2] Brother Lawrence wrote in the 17th century that if we pray with words, let it be a short phrase rather than long prayers. The Breath Prayers in this book are exactly that: Short phrases repeated in the rhythm of slow and deliberate breathing.

PRAYING PAUSE

Rest in your breathing for a moment... Become
aware of God's presence in your breathing... Now
hear God say, "I love you" on your breath in... And
say, "I love you" to God on your breath out... God
is the breath within your breathing!

Even though early Christians were not aware of the things that research has since proven, they knew how to pray this way. Breath prayers have been a part of

Christianity since its very beginning. The Desert Fathers and Mothers, a group of early Christians in the third century, went into the desert to live an austere life and transform their lives into the Life of Christ. They contemplated Christ's life in short breath prayers, like "Lord have mercy" or other phrases from the Psalms. God's word was breathed in slowly, deeply and repeatedly. This way the prayer descended from their minds into their hearts and it prayed itself, even in their sleep. Breathing a prayer to God is a powerful way to connect with the Divine.

Our breath is also a wonderful analogy for God because it is invisible yet always with us. As long as we are breathing, God is in our breathing and the more conscious we become of our breath, the more conscious we become of God. As David Frenette said, "Like God, your breath is a presence that acts, that breathes, in you. Notice your breath, present and moving in you, as a symbol of the way God's presence lives and acts in you. Observing your breath is a way of opening yourself to God, a way of responding to the gift of life."[3]

The Breath Prayers can be prayed throughout the day without adding another time commitment to your schedule. However, at first it might be difficult to remember the prayers, since you are not used to praying this way. I recommend setting a few minutes aside every morning in the first week of your practice. It is also helpful to pray the prayers at certain times during the day. You could start your lunch break with a minute of Breath Prayers or set your cell phone for certain times during the day. Newberg and Waldman found that, "The brain actually 'marks' these important rituals, and thus each time you perform them, your memory circuits will guide you into the desired state more quickly and with greater intensity."[4]

PRAYING PAUSE

> *Rest in the rhythm of your breathing for a moment... Observe your breath as if it were the first breath you ever took... Just observe... After a moment, deepen your breathing just a little...Breathe more deeply for a while... Observe how it feels... Let go and breathe naturally... Do you feel a difference?*

Breathing in God Deeply

I'll breathe my life into you and you'll live. —Ezekiel 37:14 (MSG)

In many translations of the Bible, the above quote is also translated as "I will put my Spirit in you and you will live" because the words "breath" and "spirit" are one word in Hebrew (ruah) and Greek (pneuma). After Jesus had died on the cross, he appeared to his disciples, wished them peace, showed them his hands and side, took a deep breath and breathed into his disciples, and said, "Receive the Holy Spirit" (John 20:22 MSG).

Take a moment and feel the miracle of this process: We not only replenish our earthly bodies with life-giving oxygen when we breathe, but we receive the Spirit of God. That doesn't mean anything less than God living in us! Does that also mean the deeper we breathe, the more we breathe in God? This prayer can be modified by changing the words "Breathing in God deeply" to "Breathing in love deeply," "Breathing in peace deeply," or any prayer that is meaningful to you.

By your very breathing you are praying, participating in God's grace.—Richard Rohr

~ *Breathe gently and guide your awareness to your stomach area... Put your right hand on your stomach and your left hand on your chest...*

~ *Breathe in to the count of four... On the counts of one and two feel your stomach rise... On the counts of three and four feel your chest rise... It is one continuous breath in...*

~ *Breathe out to the count of four... On the counts of one and two feel your chest relax... On the counts of three and four feel your stomach relax... It is one continuous breath out...*

~ *When you are familiar with the deeper breath, pray "Breathing in" (one, two) "God deeply" (three, four)... "Breathing out" (one, two) "completely" (three, four)... "Breathing in God deeply" (breathing in)... "Breathing out completely" (breathing out)...*

~ *Sit with your eyes lowered or closed for a few moments and become aware of your body. How do you feel?*

~ *Remember to pause often during the day and let deep, conscious breathing be your prayer today.*

PRAYER: I breathe your life into me, God. Amen.

BREATHING OUT GRATITUDE

One of them, when he realized that he was healed, turned around and came back, shouting his gratitude, glorifying God. He kneeled at Jesus' feet, so grateful.—Luke 17:15 (MSG)

Living out gratitude is essential in the spiritual and material life. If you haven't said, "Thank you" for what you have, you don't really own it in your heart – and what you don't own in your heart, you don't own at all. To live a life close to God, we have to recognize and be grateful for all of God's gifts. Being grateful connects us with life as pure gift!

We all have different ways to express our gratitude, and some of us might not really know how. If you are in the latter category, start with being grateful for the breath you breathe. If you get into the habit of replacing every thought of what you don't have with a prayer of gratitude, you will realize that you have received a lot more than you could ever imagine. Instead of focusing on the problems in life, focus on the good and count your blessings. Problems help us to overcome pride, judgment and fear. Take a moment and ask yourself how you are expressing your gratitude to God.

If the only prayer you ever say in your entire life is thank you, it will be enough.—Meister Eckhart (1260-1328)

~ *Take a moment and look around you... Are you grateful for what you see?*

~ *As you breathe in, pray "Thank you" and as you breathe out, look at the many things you can be grateful for... Stay in the rhythm of your breath even if you have to repeat what you are grateful for... Pray this way until you have named ten things you are grateful for...*

~ *As you breathe in again, let your eyes rest on one person or object and feel deep gratitude...*

~ *Now close your eyes and let ten people for whom you are grateful come to your mind... Notice who they are...*

~ *Above all, be grateful for the mystery of God and the mystery of your life...*

~ *Let gratefulness be your prayer throughout the day and rejoice in what God has given to you, despite what you may feel God has not given. Help everyone you meet today be blessed by your gratefulness.*

PRAYER: Thank you, God. Amen.

BREATHING IN GOD'S LOVE

Jesus replied: "Love the Lord your God with all your heart and with all your soul and with all your mind. This is the first and greatest commandment. And the second is like it: 'Love your neighbor as yourself.'"—Matthew 22:37-39 (MSG)

Praying the "I love you" prayer has countless blessings. By practicing Jesus' first and second commandments as quoted above, we learn to love ourselves and others in a new way. Most of us did not experience unconditional love in childhood and it is hard to know what healthy love feels like. How can we love others if we don't love ourselves?

This prayer will help you feel God's unconditional love, which accepts you exactly as you are this moment. It is particularly helpful when you feel unloved and are plagued by low self-esteem. Repeating and hearing "I love you" throughout the day will increase your self-esteem and lower the anxiety level in your life. If you experience the world through love, you will discover a world of love. Another way to pray this prayer is to simply hear God say, "I am love," or say to yourself, "I am love," in the spirit of knowing that "God is love" (1 John 4:8 NIV). Take a few minutes and think of the people who love you and feel how much you are loved.

God refuses to be known; God can only be loved.—St. John of the Cross (1542-1591)

~ *Be aware of your breathing and breathe slowly and gently... God's love is within you...*

~ *As you breathe in, hear God say, "I love you... (your name)" and feel God's love for you...*

~ *As you breathe out, pray "I love you" to God...*

~ *Practice this prayer for a few minutes and gently guide yourself back to God's love when your thoughts stray away to other topics or self-doubt...*

~ *Continue to pray this prayer during the day, feeling the truth of God's love for you...*

~ *Feel God's unconditional love today, so everyone you meet will be blessed by God's love through you.*

PRAYER: I love you. Amen.

BREATHING OUT GOD'S LOVE

Jesus said: "A new command I give you: Love one another. As I have loved you, so you must love one another."—John 13:34 (NIV)

Intercessory prayer is one of the most beautiful prayers we can pray. To pray on behalf of another fulfills Jesus' command to love one another as He has loved us. But do we really know what is best for another person? Do we really know what God's will is for ourselves, much less for someone else? Although we want our loved ones to be happy and healthy, and we intercede accordingly in our prayers, we have to take a step back and know that God is in charge of all of our lives. Only God knows what is best for our loved ones and all we need to do is lift them up into God's care.

We have to pray with our eyes on God, not on the difficulties.— Oswald Chambers (1874-1917)

~ *Be aware of your breathing and take a moment to calm your mind... You are on holy ground, about to pray for someone else...*

~ *As you breathe gently, "see" the person you want to pray for...*

~ *As you breathe in, inwardly say the name of God or Jesus...*

~ *As you breathe out, inwardly say the name of the person you pray for...*

~ *Continue this prayer in the rhythm of your breathing until you feel a sense of peace...*

~ *Let God's healing flow through you in this prayer, so your loved one will be blessed by this same healing. Let this prayer, and the knowledge that God is in charge, also be a comfort to you.*

PRAYER: Thy will be done. Amen.

BREATHING IN GOD'S STILLNESS

Be still and know that I am God.—Psalm 46:10 (NIV)

The command to "be still" comes from the Hebrew word "raphah" and means "be weak," "let go" or "release." God asks us to be weak, to let go and trust. Trusting God means letting go of our thoughts regarding the past and the future and coming into the present moment. This means we are letting go of control. God gave us free will, including the ability to choose our thoughts. If the focal point of our mind is on our busy day ahead and we live future events in the present moment, we will lose God's presence and peace. If we focus our mind on God in the given moment, we will be present in all we do and experience God's peace.

This prayer can be prayed in different situations during the day. We can pray while in traffic, during a business meeting or when picking up our kids from school. As we become aware of God's stillness throughout our day, we will be rewarded by getting everything done peacefully in God's time.

Being still does not mean don't move. It means move in peace.—E'yen A. Gardner

~ *Be aware of your breath and breathe gently...*

~ *As you breathe in, pray "Be"...*

~ *As you breathe out, pray "still"...*

~ *Feel God's stillness increase with every breath and pray "Be still" until you feel God's peace and presence...*

~ *If you are in a quiet space, sit with your eyes lowered or closed and become aware of your body. How did it feel before you prayed and how does it feel now?*

~ *Let God's stillness be your prayer today, so everyone you meet will be blessed by God's stillness in you.*

PRAYER: Be still. Amen.

BREATHING OUT GOD'S PEACE

Be still and know that I am God.—Psalm 46:10 (NIV)

"Be still and know that I am God" is my favorite verse of all the psalms. The command to "be still" comes from the Hebrew word "raphah," and means to "be weak," to "let go" or to "release." To experience God in our lives, we have to acknowledge our weakness first. From this position, we have no choice but to let go and trust that God is in control of our lives. What a different view from what society asks of us!

Often this verse is quoted as God asking us to be peaceful and trust, but it really means much more than that. Meditate for a moment on "Be weak and know that I am God" and focus on the difference of this truth. God needs our weakness to work in our lives. Peace will increase in our lives to the extend we trust in God! "Be weak..." is the most wonderful prayer to release fears and the need to always be strong and in control. This verse can be prayed in many different ways. You can pray it as a "Prayer of the Heart," where you repeat the phrase continuously. You can also pray this prayer as a Breath Prayer to connect you with God's life-giving breath and peace.

My grace is sufficient for thee: for my strength is made perfect in weakness.—2 Corinthians 12:9 (KJV)

~ *Slowly repeat the verse in the rhythm of your breath. You may shorten it if you wish, or stay with the line that works best for you. If you shorten the verse, spend as much time on one line as you wish and then move on to the next...*

~ *"Be still (breathe in) and know (breathe out) that I am (in) God (out)"...*

~ *"Be still (in) and know (out) that I (in) am (out)"...*

~ *"Be still (in) and know (out)"...*

~ *"Be (in) still (out)"...*

~ *"Be"...*

~ *Practice this prayer during the day and let God's peace be with you, so everyone you meet today will be blessed by God's peace in you.*

PRAYER: Be still and know that I am God. Amen.

BREATHING IN GOD'S HELP

When I called out, you answered me; you strengthened me.—
Psalm 138:4 (ISV)

When we ask God for help in our prayers, we acknowledge that we are not in control of our lives and that we need help. Often we think that we know what this help should look like. Have you ever perceived a life situation as terrible, only to discover later that what happened was the greatest blessing in your life?

None of us wants to suffer, and even Jesus asked to be spared suffering but he trusted God completely, expressing his humanness and at the same time asking for God's will to be done (Matthew 26:36-39).

Let us start our prayer by visualizing Jesus walking toward us, asking: "What do you want me to do for you?" (Mark 10:51 NIV). Take a deep breath and tell Jesus all you need and yearn for. Ask boldly and in detail for your desires in life. Pour out your heart and don't censor the wishes that God might have for you. When you are ready, take a deep breath and find the word that expresses your yearning closely. Continue with the following Breath Prayer and remember that God knows the wishes of your heart better than you do.

Please, LORD, rescue me! Come quickly, LORD, and help me.—Psalm 40:13 (NLT)

~ *Breathing softly, know that God is as close as your breathing...*

~ *As you breathe in, address God or Jesus in a way that expresses your relationship with God at the moment. It could be "God," "Abba," "Father," "Jesus," "Healer," "Teacher"...*

~ *As you breathe out, express to God or Jesus what you want. You can be very specific (help for a loved one, safe travels, a job, a home) or more general (peace, love, joy)... Let it be one or two words only... Breathe out your wish for the day...*

~ *Breathe gently and practice this Breath Prayer until you feel grounded in God and the present moment...*

~ *Sit with your eyes lowered or closed for a few moments and let go...*

~ *When you pray this prayer during the day, let God's presence flow through you, so everyone you meet today will be blessed by God's presence in you.*

PRAYER: Thy will be done. Amen.

BREATHING OUT GOD'S JOY

These things I have spoken to you, that my joy may be in you, and that your joy may be full.—John 15:11 (ESV)

Many Christians talk about God in a serious and sometimes fearful way and that God will punish us if we do not live in a righteous way. The word fear in the Bible is translated from the Hebrew word "yirah" and can mean to be fearful, but it also means to be in awe or full of reverence. "Fear the Lord your God" (Deuteronomy 10:20 NLT) means to be in awe of God!

God wants us to be joyful. The word joy is mentioned about 250 times in the Bible. We are asked to "shout for joy" (Psalm 20:5 NIV), "let us rejoice today and be glad" (Psalm 118:24 NIV), "have a cheerful heart because it is good medicine" (Proverbs 17:22 NIV), "know that the joy of the Lord is our strength" (Nehemiah 8:10 NIV), and "rejoice and no one will take away our joy" (John 16:22 NIV). Living joyfully and appreciating God's world is a beautiful spiritual discipline to engage in because living joyfully is worshiping God.

Joy is the infallible sign of the presence of God.—Pierre Teilhard de Chardin (1881-1955)

~ *Be aware of your breath and be present... There is so much to be joyous about...*

~ *As you breathe in, pray "God is present"...*

~ *As you breathe out, pray "God is joy"...*

~ *As you breathe in, pray "I am present"...*

~ *As you breathe out, pray "I rejoice" and smile...*

~ *Breathe slowly and stay with this four-breath rhythm until you feel God's joy...*

~ *Let God's joy be your prayer today, so everyone you meet will be blessed by God's joy in you.*

PRAYER: God is present. God is joy. I am present.
I rejoice. Amen.

BREATHING IN GOD'S HEALING

You're asking the wrong question. You're looking for someone to blame. There is no such cause-effect here. Look instead for what God can do.—John 9:2-3 (MSG)

Knowing the goodness of God makes us ask why there is so much pain and suffering in the world. Even Jesus had to endure terrible pain and cried out, "My God, my God, why have you forsaken me?"(Mark 15:34 NIV). We too, like Jesus, cry out at times "Why?" and "Why me?"

The first step to God's healing is to accept that pain is part of being human and that it is not God's punishment! Pain, whether it is physical, emotional or spiritual, can be an opportunity for God's deeper healing. The pain we are experiencing today might prevent deeper pain in the future. It might be God's loving way of gradually adjusting our life into God's life. God has given us free will and many of us unknowingly stray from what is best for us.

To experience pain in our life is not a choice, but suffering is a choice. If we accept pain as one life experience among others, we can prevent suffering in our life.

In my own life, I think I can honestly say that out of the deepest pain has come the strongest conviction of the presence of God and the love of God.—Elisabeth Elliot (1926-2015)

~ *As you breathe deeply, come into the moment...*

~ *Gently detach from the negative association you might have with the word "pain." Feel the physical or emotional sensation and let tears flow, if they need to flow... As you breathe gently, release any tension...*

~ *On your breath in, say "I trust," and on your breath out, "in God's healing"... God will guide you through this...*

~ *You may also want to picture yourself touching the hem of Jesus' garment, hearing Jesus say, "Daughter [or son], your faith has made you well. Go in peace. Your suffering is over" (Mark 5:34 NLT)...*

~ *Sit with your eyes lowered or closed for a few moments and know God's grace and healing is taking place right now within you... Stay present in the moment, relax and participate in God's healing...*

PRAYER: I trust in God's healing. Amen.

BREATHING OUT GOD'S FORGIVENESS

*"Receive the Holy Spirit," he said. "If you forgive someone's sins, they're gone for good. If you don't forgive sins, what are you going to do with them?"—*John 20:22-23 (MSG)

*In prayer there is a connection between what God does and what you do. You can't get forgiveness from God, for instance, without also forgiving others.—*Matthew 6:14-15 (MSG)

*And why worry about a speck in your friend's eye when you have a log in your own?... First get rid of the log in your own eye; then you will see well enough to deal with the speck in your friend's eye.—*Luke 6:41-42 (NLT)

Forgiveness is one of the most complex spiritual concepts to understand. Jesus has taught us everything we need to know about forgiveness. Meditating regularly on the three scripture verses above will bring us to a place of understanding, peace and forgiveness. Forgiveness then becomes a way of life.

Break the cycle of endless pain, anger and negativity that keeps you captive by forgiving self and others. Forgiveness frees the one who forgives!

*To be a Christian means to forgive the inexcusable because God has forgiven the inexcusable in you.—*C.S. Lewis (1898-1963)

~ *Become aware of your breathing and allow the steady rhythm of your breath bring you to a place of calm and quiet...*

~ *As you gently breathe in say, "I forgive you," or "I am willing to forgive," or "God's forgiveness." Choose words that are right for you and the person you want to forgive. It is a process...*

~ *Breathing out, gently say the name of the person you need to forgive...*

~ *Continue with this prayer until you feel your heart soften... You might have to pick it back up and need to forgive again, and again... True forgiveness has its own rhythm and can't be rushed...*

~ *Sit with your eyes lowered or closed for a few moments and allow your awareness to rest in your breathing and God's forgiveness.*

PRAYER: I am willing to forgive. Amen.

BREATHING THE JESUS PRAYER

But the tax collector stood at a distance. He would not even look up to heaven, but beat his breast and said, "God, have mercy on me, a sinner."—Luke 18:13 (NIV)

The Jesus Prayer is an ancient form of prayer that goes back to early Christianity. It is also called a "Prayer of the Heart," where the words "Lord Jesus Christ, Son of God, have mercy on me, a sinner" are continuously repeated in the mind until the words sink into the heart and become a joyous praise on their own. The most beautiful account of the Jesus Prayer is described by an anonymous 19th-century Russian Christian in the book *The Way of a Pilgrim*. The pilgrim practiced the Jesus Prayer while he walked across Russia.

The Jesus Prayer can also be prayed as a Breath Prayer. The words are said in the rhythm of your breath. For some people, the word "sinner" doesn't work and they have replaced it with "seeker." Praying the Jesus Prayer as a Breath Prayer connects you with your breath and adds a physical dimension to it. It is also a wonderful experience to pray this prayer while walking and experiencing the pilgrim aspect of it.

Rejoice always, pray continually, give thanks in all circumstances; for this is God's will for you in Christ Jesus.
—1 Thessalonians 5:16-18

~ *Be aware of your breathing for a moment and deepen it slightly...*

~ *As you breathe in, say, "Lord Jesus Christ"...*

~ *As you breathe out, say, "Son of God"...*

~ *As you breathe in, say, "Have mercy on me"...*

~ *As you breathe out, "A sinner (seeker)"...*

~ *When you pray this Breath Prayer during the day, feel Jesus' mercy flow through you into the world.*

PRAYER: Lord Jesus Christ, Son of God, have mercy on me, a sinner (seeker). Amen.

BREATHING THE LORD'S PRAYER

Jesus said: "This, then, is how you should pray."—Matthew 6:9 (NIV)

When the disciples asked Jesus how to pray, he answered: "And when you pray, do not keep on babbling like pagans, for they think they will be heard because of their many words. Do not be like them, for your Father knows what you need before you ask him" (Matthew 6:7-8 NIV). Jesus advised us to pray with few words because God already knows the desire of our hearts. The Lord's Prayer is one of the most beautiful prayers; however, if we have known a prayer for a long time, we often say the words without feeling its meaning. We need to pray it with a new consciousness every so often. If you pray the words of the Lord's Prayer slowly and in the rhythm of your breathing, they will take on a fresh and new meaning.

If a man, in praying that prayer, were to be stopped by every word until he had thoroughly prayed it, it would take him a lifetime."—Henry Ward Beecher (1813-1887)

~ *Breathing in, pray:*   Our Father in heaven

~ *Breathing out, pray:*   hallowed be your name

~ *Breathing in, pray:*   your kingdom come

~ *Breathing out, pray:*   your will be done

~ *Breathing in, pray:*   on earth

~ *Breathing out, pray:*   as it is in heaven.

~ *Breathing in, pray:*   Give us today

~ *Breathing out, pray:*   our daily bread.

~ *Breathing in, pray:*   And forgive us our debts,

~ *Breathing out, pray:*   as we also have forgiven our debtors.

~ *Breathing in, pray:*   And lead us not into temptation

~ *Breathing out, pray:*   but deliver us from evil. Amen.

THE BODY AWARENESS PRAYERS

Christ has no body now on earth but yours.
—St. Teresa of Avila (1515-1582)

The human body is a miracle. The fact that we breathe, our hearts beat, our legs walk, our arms hug, our minds think, our eyes see, our ears hear and our skin feels is a miracle of God!

PRAYING PAUSE

> *Come into the present moment and feel the*
> *miracle of your body... You are alive now...*

Our bodies are always in the present moment of where we are in time and space. Our minds wander off into the future and into the past but our bodies are always in the present moment. Once we are aware of it, it is one of those simple yet profound and eye-opening truths that can change our lives.

PRAYING PAUSE

> *Rest in your body for a moment and feel yourself*
> *relaxing into the moment... Your body is always*
> *in the present moment of where you are...*

Becoming aware of our body keeps us in the present moment, and also in the presence of God because our body is "a sacred place, the place of the Holy Spirit" (1 Corinthians 6:19 MSG). The more we practice the presence of God by being aware of our body, the more we take our energy away from our thinking, meaning the past and the future. We will then be truly in the present moment, acting within God's presence and not our own agenda.

PRAYING PAUSE

> *"Or do you not know that your body is the temple of the Holy Spirit who is in you, whom you have from God, and you are not your own?"*
> *— 1 Corinthians 6:19 (NKJV)*

> *Meditate on the Bible quote for a moment by rereading the question slowly several times... Let this truth move from your head into your heart...*

If our mind takes all our attention, this connection is not possible. When we are completely identified with our mind, we are cutting ourselves off from God's holy presence within us. Then it is "my will" all the way and there is no room for God's will, which is deeply rooted within us. When we keep some of our awareness in our body, we will come to know God's presence in us in ever deeper ways. God's "gentle whisper" (1 Kings 19:11-13 NIV) is speaking in the depth of our body and soul, waiting to be heard. John O'Donohue expresses this truth by calling the body "...a sacrament. A sacrament is a visible sign of invisible grace... The body is a sacred threshold; and it deserves to be respected, minded and understood in its spiritual nature."[1]

PRAYING PAUSE

> *"Therefore honor God with your bodies."*
> *—1 Corinthians 6:20 (NIV)*
>
> *Rest in the moment and allow your body to relax... Soften your face and relax your jaw... Relax your shoulders and your stomach... Honor God with your body... What does that mean to you?... Meditate on the scripture for a moment...*

The Body Awareness prayers help us to honor our body and God's miraculous Being within us. Our body is extremely truthful and reflects what is going on in our life. We might think that we are content and happy in a certain situation, but our body might show us otherwise. Our thoughts can betray us and even our feelings reflect only the truth of our state of mind at that moment, but our body teaches a deeper truth. If we stay connected to our body, we will learn how to connect to the spirit within.

The body is not only the temple of God, keeping us grounded in the present moment, but we also experience God's presence through our senses.

According to Frederick Buechner, "It is not just to our minds that God makes himself known, because, whatever we may think, we are much more than just our minds, but to our sense of touch and taste too, to our seeing and hearing and smelling the air whether it is laden with burning incense leaves or baking bread or honest human sweat. 'O taste and see that the Lord is good!' says the 34th Psalm, and it not just being metaphorical."[2] John O'Donohue adds an interesting point to the importance of being aware of our senses: "By being attuned to the wisdom of your senses, you will never become an exile in your own life, an outsider lost in an external spiritual place that your will and intellect have constructed."[3]

To fully live into our life, we have to reclaim the sacredness of the body and remember that God works in the world through our physical incarnation.

PRAYING PAUSE

Become aware of your breathing and feel the sacredness of your body... Feel the temperature of the air... The clothes touching your body... Your body touching the chair or couch you sit on... Feel the sensation of being a body in this world...

Christ has no body but yours,
No hands, no feet on earth but yours,
Yours are the eyes with which he looks

Compassion on this world,
Yours are the feet with which he walks to do
*   good,*
Yours are the hands, with which he blesses all
*   the world.*
Yours are the hands, yours are the feet,
Yours are the eyes, you are his body.
Christ has no body now but yours,
No hands, no feet on earth but yours,
Yours are the eyes with which he looks
Compassion on this world.
Christ has no body now on earth but yours.

—St. Teresa of Avila (1515-1582)

BREATH AWARENESS

Then the Lord God formed a man from the dust of the ground and breathed into his nostrils the breath of life and the man became a living being.—Genesis 2:7 (NIV)

This prayer is especially helpful when your thoughts are going in many different directions and you have difficulties calming your mind even with meditation and prayer. By concentrating your awareness on the inside of your nose, you leave no room for other activities in your mind and you will relax immediately because you breathe more deeply. You will also become aware of the moment when the air becomes part of your body and you are breathing in the Holy Spirit of God. Remember the words "spirit" and "breath" are the same word in Greek and Hebrew. We are all breathing in the same air and the same spirit. We truly are one body in Christ through our breath!

Feelings come and go like clouds in a windy sky. Conscious breathing is my anchor.—Thich Nhat Hanh

~ *As you breathe deeply and gently, become aware of the tip of your nose. Locate a spot inside your nose where you can feel the air entering your body... How is the air temperature?*

~ *As you breathe out, become aware of the air leaving your body through the tip of your nose... How is the temperature?*

~ *Leave your awareness at the tip of your nose while gently breathing and feeling God's "breath of life"...*

~ *When your thoughts stray away, gently and without judgment guide your awareness back to the tip of your nose...*

~ *Instead of concentrating on the tip of your nose, you can also concentrate on the pause between your in and out breath...*

~ *Practice the prayer several times during the day and be aware of God's breath within your breathing.*

PRAYER: I breathe God's breath of life. Amen.

BREATHE, LISTEN, WATCH

When Jacob awoke from his sleep, he thought, "Surely the
LORD is in this place, and I was not aware of it."—Genesis
28:16 (NIV)

It is likely none of us wants to feel the way Jacob felt,
but like Jacob, we often are not aware of God's presence.
Our thoughts dwell in the past and the future instead of
in the present moment. Staying present is one of the
most difficult things for us adults to do, although we
knew how to as children. Let's tap into this knowledge
and become present again.

Notice that there is a power other than your
thoughts that can change your awareness from your
thoughts to your senses. This is your physical
connection to God within you. Whenever you feel
disconnected from your life and God, turn to this prayer
with an attitude of worship and the assurance that God
is right here with you. If you stay present using your
senses, you will always be connected to your life and
God's life within you and all around you.

Yes. I'll stay with you, I'll protect you wherever you go, and I'll
bring you back to this ground. I'll stick with you until I've
done everything I promised you.—Genesis 28:15 (MSG)

~ *Breathe gently and simply observe your breathing... No need to control your breath... Breathe in God's presence and breath...*

~ *When your mind strays, listen to what you hear... Simply listen without attaching a meaning to the sound...*

~ *When your mind wanders again, guide your awareness to your surroundings... Simply see...*

~ *Alternate between observing your breathing, listening, and being aware of your surroundings when your thoughts take you away from the present moment... Pray this way until you are present and calm...*

~ *Can you feel the power within that guides your awareness? How does it feel?*

~ *When you pray this way during the day, you will become present to God's guidance and promise in your life.*

PRAYER: I am aware of God's presence. Amen.

BRUSHING YOUR TEETH

It's not what goes into your mouth that defiles you; you are defiled by the words that come out of your mouth.—Matthew 15:11 (NLT)

Healthy teeth are very important to our overall health. Toothpaste companies promise us that a particular brand will keep our teeth white and our breath fresh, but if our words are not kind and true, how can our breath be pure?

Many of us perceive the time of brushing our teeth as a necessary but not particularly joyous time. With the right attitude, though, it can become a prayerful and joyous anchor at the beginning and end of every day. If you let this time become a prayer, your teeth will thank you by staying healthy and your words will honor God and life.

Words which do not give the light of Christ increase the darkness.—Mother Teresa (1910-1997)

~ *When you pick up your toothbrush, take a deep, deliberate breath...*

~ *When you spread toothpaste on your brush, be aware of the amount of paste you put on. Appreciate the smooth texture and enjoy the beauty and smell of it...*

~ *Look at your teeth and feel the motion of your brush... Watch the brush circling your teeth and the paste cleansing the surface of your teeth... Be patient with yourself and come back to the present moment when your thoughts stray... If it helps you to stay present, recite the prayer below while you brush your teeth...*

~ *Say the prayer as you put your toothbrush away in the morning...*

~ *When you put your brush away at night, ask yourself whether you have lived into the prayer during the day.*

PRAYER: May only goodness and truth come out of my mouth today. Amen.

DRINKING A CUP OF COFFEE OR TEA

I'll lift the cup of salvation – a toast to God!—Psalm 116:13 (MSG)

When you drink your first cup of coffee or tea in the morning, allow yourself to appreciate it in a new way. By being present in your daily routine, you make the ordinary holy.

The way you start your day is important because it shapes your day. If you rush into it, you will rush the whole day. If you become aware of God's presence early in the morning, God's light will shine in you throughout the day.

I take my morning mug of coffee in both hands and lift it ever so slightly toward the sky... In itself it is nothing. But partaken with mindfulness, it is a small act of worship, an act of consecration, a prayer of thankfulness to the awakening day.—Kent Nerburn

~ *When you pick up your cup of coffee or tea, breathe fully and enjoy the fragrance of your beverage... Feel your hands touching the cup...*

~ *Notice how the cup touches your lips and the liquid fills your mouth... When your thoughts stray, come back to the present moment by tasting the coffee or tea...*

~ *Become aware of the presence of God while you are drinking your coffee or tea...*

~ *Lift your heart and cup toward heaven and be receptive to God's presence in this small act of worship...*

~ *Continue worshiping this way throughout the day, enjoying every beverage with gratitude.*

PRAYER: I lift the cup of salvation. Amen.

EATING

Go, eat your bread with joy, and drink your wine with a merry heart, for God has already approved what you do.
—Ecclesiastes 9:7 (NIV)

Breathing and eating are sacred activities in similar ways because we are taking something inside of us and using it for our nourishment. As a culture, we don't really honor our food anymore, but judge it by how many calories it has or whether it is fat-free. We eat healthfully because we "should," and are guilt ridden if we occasionally eat chocolate or ice cream.

If you eat your food with love, chew slowly and eat the right amount, you can eat whatever your heart and body desire. You might want to change some of your eating habits and take a break to eat instead of eating while you work. Or eat only while you sit and make it a holy habit to have family meals or meals with friends.

Be present today; celebrate God and the food God has provided for you and work up "a good appetite for God. He's food and drink in the best meal you'll ever eat" (Matthew 5:6 MSG).

There is no mystery in why Jesus chose a meal to reveal his death to those he loved, why he chose a meal to commemorate his truth.—Kent Nerburn

~ When you sit down to eat, breathe deeply and look at your food for a moment instead of eating immediately... Enjoy the colors and the delicious smell... Pray in a way that is meaningful to you... It doesn't have to be in words...

~ When you take the first bite of food, truly taste your food and chew slowly...

~ Continue to eat slowly and prayerfully and enjoy every bite... Stop eating when you feel full. You can always eat more food at another time...

~ When you eat, ask yourself once in a while whether you are eating out of habit or trying to fill an emotional void...

~ When you are finished eating, take a moment and thank God for the food and the hands that grew and prepared it...

~ Let slow, deliberate and joyful eating be your prayer today.

PRAYER: I eat my bread with joy and drink my wine with a merry heart. Amen.

FEELING

Jesus wept.—John 11:35 (NIV)

The Body Awareness Prayers would not be complete without a prayer on "feeling." Many of us act out of old emotional patterns to a situation in the present and do not react to the topic at hand. Feelings are a wonderful indicator of how God is present in our lives.

As spiritual beings we think that we have to be joyous and positive all the time, but as human beings we have negative feelings as well. The "human Jesus" was angry, fearful, and sad! We have to honor our emotional life because our life is shaped by how we feel about ourselves.

When we live close to God, it is less about what we have to face today, but instead how we feel about ourselves while we face it. Spiritual growth happens when we are true to who we are at the moment. It is important to love and accept ourselves the way we are because then God will be able to help us with any changes we need to make.

When you come to know yourselves, then you will become known, and you will realize that it is you who are the sons of the living Father. But if you will not know yourselves, you dwell in poverty and it is you who are that poverty. —Coptic Gospel of Thomas #3

~ *Rest in your breathing... How are you feeling right now? How does your body feel?... Do not judge, simply observe...*

~ *When you are with people today, ask yourself how you feel in their presence... Be aware of the signals your body gives you in the presence of others because your body does not deceive you...*

~ *Pause often during the day and notice how you are feeling... Do not judge your feelings, simply observe. If you are unhappy, ask yourself: What makes me happy and joyous in life? Do I need to change the situation or do I need to change my attitude and thoughts?*

~ *Let God's presence shine through you by being aware of how you feel today.*

PRAYER: I am aware of my feelings. Amen.

LISTENING

Are you listening to this? Really listening?—Mark 4:23 (MSG)

St. John of the Cross said, "God's first language is silence." So how do we listen to God if God doesn't speak to us in words? We need to learn to listen to God's "gentle whisper" in creation and in the events of our lives. God speaks to us in the joyous and painful moments.

Listening to God involves more than our ears; it involves our hearts and the ability to detach from our own agenda. When our attention is taken up by thinking about our response in a conversation, our minds are so busy that we only hear our own thoughts.

Let's take a moment each day to listen to the birds sing or the wind whistle in the trees. And let's take time every so often and listen to God's "gentle whisper" in silence. True listening is worship. How do you listen to God?

To truly listen is to risk being changed forever.—James (Sakej) Youngblood Henderson

~ Breathing gently, listen to the sounds around you...
Do not engage your mind by identifying the sounds,
only listen...

~ Be aware of the singing of the birds today. They sing
their song of praise whether someone is listening or
not...

~ Listen for God in a piece of music. You might want to
close your eyes...

~ Listen for God's voice as you talk with a loved one,
co-worker or stranger... If your thoughts cause your
mind to wander, gently and without judgment guide
yourself back to listening...

~ Whenever you need to make a decision, or feel
nervous or off-center, breathe deeply and listen to the
gentle whisper within...

~ Pause during the day and give yourself the gift of
listening for God's voice in all of life and share the
blessing of God's presence.

PRAYER: I listen for the voice of God in all of life. Amen.

OPENING OUR HANDS

May the favor of the Lord our God rest on us; establish the work of our hands for us —yes, establish the work of our hands.—Psalm 90:17 (NIV)

The German philosopher Immanuel Kant said that the hand is the visible expression of the mind. We express our thoughts and emotions with our hands. We work with our hands. We pray with our hands. And we touch with our hands. Notice how many things you do with your hands today and you will be amazed by the importance of your hands.

Our hands are a wonderful image for our spiritual journey. When our hands are closed or filled with things, we cannot receive new gifts. When our minds are closed and filled, we cannot receive God.

Let's become people with open and empty hands, able to receive God's blessings moment by moment. Let our hands teach us today how to keep an open mind by turning them up to heaven, affirming that all the gifts come from God. Come with empty hands before God and let them be filled with love, peace and joy every moment of your day.

Bless to me, O God, My heart and my speech, And bless to me, O God, The handling of my hands. —Celtic Morning Prayer

~ *Breathe gently, and become aware of your hands...*
Feel your hands without looking at them... Imagine
for a moment what it would be like to live without
hands...

~ *Slowly and consciously open your eyes and look at*
your hands... Turn your hands around and look at the
inside of your hands... God works through your
hands...

~ *Slowly open your hands toward heaven and breathe*
into the openness of your hands... Give everything
that bothers you to God, raising your hands...

~ *Fold your hands in prayer and then refold them with*
the other thumb on top... Feel into your folded
hands...

~ *Be aware of the miracle and work of your hands*
today... Throughout the day, do everything with an
awareness of the presence of God in your hands...

~ *With gratitude in your heart, let your hands be your*
silent, trusting prayer today, bringing God's love into
the world.

PRAYER: May God bless the work of my hands. Amen.

RELAXING

I said to myself, "Relax and rest. God has showered you with blessings."—Psalm 116:7 (MSG)

One of the biggest hurdles to prayer is nervous tension and the inability to quiet the mind. If we want to connect with God, we must learn to quiet ourselves. This quietness is already a form of prayer in itself because we are connecting with God's "still, small voice" within.

One way to quiet the mind is to become aware of and relax our bodies. When we focus our minds on our bodies, our minds automatically calm and quiet because our bodies are always in the peaceful present moment where "I AM" resides.

Most of us hold physical tension in our jaws, shoulders and abdomens. Often, after we have relaxed our jaw, we discover that it has already tensed up again by the time we have relaxed our stomachs. Relaxing jaw, shoulders and abdomen will help you be present in your body. Jesus asks us to follow him and "take a real rest. Walk with me and work with me – watch how I do it. Learn the unforced rhythms of grace" (Matthew 11:28 MSG). Even though we might not be able to follow Jesus to the mountaintop, we can follow Jesus by relaxing into the moment and resting this way.

Take rest; a field that has rested gives bountiful crop.—Ovid, Roman poet (43 BC-AD 18)

~ *Breathe gently and become aware of your body...*

~ *Relax your jaw... Your shoulders... Your abdomen... Feel your whole body relax...*

~ *Be aware of the places where your body touches the chair... Sink into the chair and let go... Let your body be held by the chair and let God hold you... You are held in the palm of God's hand...*

~ *Breathe into this restful moment and relax your jaw, your shoulders and your abdomen again... And again...*

~ *Sit with your eyes lowered or closed for a moment and enjoy the peace in body, mind and soul... God is taking care of you!*

~ *When you pause and relax during the day, do so with an attitude of humble worship because "you, yourself are God's temple" (1 Corinthians 3:17 NIV).*

PRAYER: I relax and rest in God. Amen.

SEEING

Your eyes are windows into your body. If you open your eyes wide in wonder and belief, your body fills up with light. If you live squinty-eyed in greed and distrust, your body is a dark cellar.—Matthew 6:22-23 (MSG)

Our eyes can look at the world in many different ways: we can have a fearful, greedy, judgmental, resentful, indifferent, hateful or loving perspective. Take a deep breath and ask yourself: How do I look at the world? Are your eyes Christ's eyes and do you look "compassion on this world" as Teresa of Avila calls it?

The way we see the world shapes our life. If we want to see clearly, our mind has to be still and not be preoccupied with the past or the future; otherwise, all we see are problems. We could see the most beautiful sunset and not be touched by it because our heart is closed and our mind is negative. I believe that is what Jesus meant when he asked us, "Do you have eyes but fail to see?" (Mark 8:18 NIV). Another reason why we might fail to see is the familiarity of our world. We are used to the beauty around us, whether it be our family and friends or the beauty of nature.

In truth, worse than not seeing at all is seeing but not being touched by what you see.—Mark Nepo

~ *Close your eyes for a moment and when you open them, feel the miracle that you can open your eyes... And see... What if you had never seen this before?... What if you would never see it again?...*

~ *Take a gentle breath and look around you... Are you grateful for what you see?...*

~ *Look at a loved one's face with new eyes... Put your thoughts on hold and look into their face and discover who they truly are...*

~ *Look at a stranger as if you were looking into Jesus' eyes...*

~ *Look at yourself today with loving and compassionate eyes...*

~ *Take a moment during the day to look at something in nature and enjoy the beauty of God's creation...*

~ *Make it your prayer today to see the familiar with unfamiliar eyes.*

PRAYER: My eyes are open in wonder and belief. Amen.

SMILING

And what a relief to see your friendly smile. It is like seeing the face of God!—Genesis 33:10 (NLT)

Smiling and smiles create happiness. When we smile, we relax hundreds of muscles in our face. Even if we fake a smile, it starts a biochemical reaction and our brain releases happiness-generating chemicals into our system. Smiling repeatedly helps to interrupt mood disorders and strengthens the brain's neural ability to maintain a positive outlook on life. Smiling stimulates brain circuits that enhance social interaction, empathy and mood.

When we smile, people around us will react with kindness and generosity and everyone will feel better in the exchange. Didn't Jesus ask us to love God and love our neighbor as self? Our smile expresses our love and makes the world a happier place one person at a time. As Mother Teresa said, "Peace begins with a smile."

Make ready for the Christ whose smile, like lightning, sets free the song of everlasting glory that now sleeps, in your paper flesh, like dynamite.—Thomas Merton (1915-1968)

~ *When you awaken, smile and remember that you are created in the image of God...*

~ *When you talk to somebody, smile and show the face of God...*

~ *When you pay your bills, smile and show the face of God...*

~ *When you are on the phone, smile and show the face of God...*

~ *When you make the bed, smile and show the face of God...*

~ *When you drive a car, smile and show the face of God...*

~ *When you work on the computer, smile and show the face of God...*

~ *When you look into the mirror, smile and see the face of God.*

PRAYER: I smile. Amen.

TAKING A SHOWER

I'll pour pure water over you and scrub you clean. I'll give you a new heart, put a new spirit in you. —Ezekiel 36:25 (MSG)

Have you ever felt that taking a shower has not only cleansed your body but also renewed your spirit? Is your mind present when you take a shower?

Often we are not one in body, mind and spirit. While we shower, we think about our to-do list or engage in negative self-talk about our body. How often do we absentmindedly and judgmentally wash our body without being aware of God's presence in it? Our body is always in the present moment with God and being aware of it while we take a shower will bring us into the holy presence of God. If we experience the shower as a time of oneness and prayer, it will not only cleanse our body but also give us a new heart and spirit.

Do you not know that your bodies are temples of the Holy Spirit, who is in you, whom you have received from God?... Therefore honor God with your bodies. —1 Corinthians 6:19-20 (NIV)

~ When you turn on the water, become aware of the preciousness of water and the privilege of being able to take a shower...

~ Step into the shower, take a deep breath and stand under the water for a few seconds, enjoying its warmth...

~ Feel the places where the water touches your body... Watch the water pearl down your skin... Listen to the sound of it... Smell the fragrance of the soap... Be present in your body, mind and soul...

~ Gently wash and caress your body... Enjoy the bubbles of the soap... Massage your face... Lovingly wash your stomach...

~ Continue to be present in your body, mind and soul as you dry your body.

PRAYER: I receive a new heart and spirit. Amen.

TOUCHING

And whoever touched him was healed.—Matthew 14:36
(MSG)

When we touch somebody, we communicate love, tenderness, belonging and warmth. Touch opens us, heals us and fosters self-confidence and self-worth. We all need to touch and to be touched. There are many ways we can enjoy touch and, from a therapeutic perspective, there is nothing more healing. We can also be "touched" when we are emotionally moved by an experience. We even say, "That touches my soul." As the verse from Matthew illustrates, Jesus healed many people by touching them and by being touched by them, not only physically but also emotionally and spiritually.

Whatever else we are, we are bodies and that as bodies we need to touch and be touched by each other.—Frederick Buechner

~ *Take a deep, deliberate breath and settle into your body... Feel the surface you sit on... Feel the air around you... Feel the sound touch your ears... Feel the sights touch your eyes...*

~ *Touch whatever is close to you... How does it feel? Smooth, soft, rough...*

~ *Touch a loved one today like you have never touched them before...*

~ *Embrace and hug somebody today... If it's appropriate, touch somebody's shoulder while you talk with them...*

~ *Become aware of your sense of touch... Are you alive and awakened to the sense of touch both as sensuous, tender and healing?... Become aware of how you touch, hug and embrace...*

~ *Let your prayer be your gentle touch today.*

PRAYER: I feel God's loving touch today. Amen.

WALKING

For in Him we live and move and have our being. —Acts 17:28 (NIV)

The Christian prayer tradition of walking the labyrinth started in the fourth century and has had a strong revival in recent years. Walking the labyrinth is both a physical and spiritual experience and can be understood as a symbol for our journey through life and into the heart of God. We can integrate this beautiful tradition into our daily lives by walking prayerfully every day.

We often hurriedly walk from one place to another, in a rush to get to the next place. We arrive stressed, out of breath and on edge. However, if we stay in the present moment with our thoughts and feel our feet touching the ground, we will arrive as quickly and will be noticeably more relaxed and peaceful.

Reciting, "In God we live and move and have our being" can help us stay in the presence of God and our surroundings while we walk. When we are stressed, taking a short walk can calm our minds and provide a moment of meditative awareness of God's beauty and presence in the world.

Your entire life journey ultimately consists of the step you are taking at this moment. —Eckhart Tolle

~ *While still sitting, become aware of your legs and appreciate them for all the miraculous work they do for you every day...*

~ *Slowly get up... Feel every movement you make...*

~ *Before you take the first step, breathe deeply and be aware that you are about to take a step you have never taken before...*

~ *Take a few steps... Feel your feet touch the ground and lift up again...*

~ *Be aware of the steps you take today, going from one place to another... Breathe deeply as you walk slowly and deliberately... You might want to pray, "In God I live and move and have my being," or the beautiful Celtic prayer, "I on Thy path O God, Thou O God, in my steps."*

~ *Continue your walk with God throughout the day and let calm and deliberate walking be your prayer today.*

PRAYER: In God I live and move and have my being. Amen.

THE DAILY AWARENESS PRAYERS

We may ignore, but we can nowhere evade
the presence of God. The world is crowded with Him.
He walks everywhere incognito.
—C.S. Lewis (1898-1963)

One of my favorite quotes is by Frederick Buechner: "The place God calls you to is the place where your deep gladness and the world's deep hunger meet." I have made it my life principle in all I do. I find it easy to have deep gladness when I think of some of the "big topics," like my health, family or career; however, it can be more difficult regarding the mundane "little things." There are many tasks that are repetitive and not necessarily "joyful": making beds, cooking meals, cleaning the house, going to the office, driving in traffic, answering emails, conducting meetings and on and on the list goes.

PRAYING PAUSE

> *"The same task. Again. And again. In my bones*
> *and my blisters I feel the weight of obedience to*
> *the sameness which is unavoidable in all our*
> *lives."—Paula D'Arcy*

Breathe lightly and relax your jaw, shoulders and abdomen... In your mind (or on paper) go through a typical day and become aware of all the daily chores you have to do... Are you joyously doing them or are you bored and resentful? Do not judge yourself, only notice...

If we live our days burdened by the sameness of our many tasks, how can we live a life that is joyous and full of meaning? After all, aren't our days what our lives are made of?

In his beautiful book *Small Graces*, Kent Nerburn writes, "For though we may not live a holy life, we live in a world with holy moments."[2] And I dare say that we can make any moment into a holy moment if we live in the present and embrace all of life. To be able to deal with serious hardships in a peaceful and spiritually mature way, we have to practice the discipline of accepting all our daily tasks, disappointments and setbacks. As a spiritual director, I believe that "Where is God in this event of your life?" is the most crucial question to ask. Often, it is a surprise how quickly the answer is discovered. Whenever we encounter a negative or painful event during the day, we need to look for the lesson and the positive instead of being burdened, defeated or paralyzed by it.

PRAYING PAUSE

"It is often these minor setbacks that draw you away from My Presence. When you reframe setbacks as opportunities, you find that you gain much more than you have lost."—Sarah Young

Feel God's presence in your breath... How do you deal with disappointments and setbacks during the day?... Take a moment to pray on this question.

If the presence of God can only be experienced in the present moment, why is it so difficult for us to joyfully live in that same present moment? Eckhart Tolle writes, "The compulsion to live almost exclusively through memory and anticipation arises because the past gives you an identity and the future holds the promise of salvation, of fulfillment in whatever form. Both are illusions."[3] I think that is an interesting way to explain our inability to stay focused. It certainly rings true when we look at children. They know how to live in the moment because they don't have a past to dwell on or a future to worry about, since their parents are taking care of them. Another way to look at it is that when we stay in our mind or ego (which perceives the past and the future), we feel in control of life because we are following "my will." When we stay in the present, we feel out of control because we are coming out of our mind or ego. We are then in fact saying, "Thy will be done."

PRAYING PAUSE

"Life is what happens while you are busy making other plans."—John Lennon (1940-1980)

Rest in the steadiness of your breathing for a moment... God provides your breath moment by moment... You are only alive at this moment... Stay in this beautiful moment and don't make any other plans...

At times when our lives are joyless and feel like drudgery, we are not living in the present moment. We are in our minds, busy making other plans or pondering problems that we cannot solve right now. A sure sign of being fully present is feeling lighthearted and joyful in what we are doing.

PRAYING PAUSE

"Joy is the infallible sign of the presence of God." —Pierre Teilhard de Chardin (1881-1955)

Does this ring true for you? Meditate on this quote for a moment before you read on and remember a joyous event in your life...

If we live in the present, God will convert moments of unloved chores into moments of joy. I experienced that truth when I came into the present while repairing the boathouse roof. I suddenly felt God's joy within me and I continued working happily, though I had been resentful before. Remember Paula D'Arcy's quote, "In my bones and my blisters I feel the weight of obedience to the sameness which is unavoidable in all our lives"? I can only assume she had a similar moment when she transitioned from those negative feelings to the following: "And then, in a single moment, I am flooded with love... I am still tired and hungry and doubtful of ever reaching my spot, yet this love picks me up and I am in its grip. I see how God honors simple obedience to our smallest tasks. I feel love all over me. Above me. Beneath me."[4]

It doesn't matter how we approach this feeling of love, whether we call it coming into the present moment, coming from the left brain into the right, or out of the head and into the heart. The fact is, we are coming into the presence of something bigger than we are, which I call the presence of God.

PRAYING PAUSE

"In the dew of little things, the heart finds its morning and is refreshed."—Kahlil Gibran (1883-1931)

Feel the joy of being alive... Watch your breathing for a moment... What little thing would give you joy right now?... Answer this question meditatively and go do it... (It took me a moment to find, but it is taking a bath, which I will do right now!)

Only when we have learned to be joyous about the little things in life, like having a meal with family and friends, seeing a sunrise, hearing a bird sing, or even folding the laundry, will we truly live. If we are not joyous in the present moment, we will not be joyous in the future either because then the future will be the Now.

The Daily Awareness Prayers help us stay in the present. Some of them engage our senses because they keep our wandering mind focused on what we are doing. Our senses bring us back into the present moment because "blessed are your eyes, for they see, and your ears, for they hear" (Matthew 13:16 NIV). However, if we are preoccupied with future problems or past pain, we "have eyes to see but do not see and ears to hear but do not hear" (Ezekiel 12:2 NIV).

The prayers help you to experience repetitive daily tasks, like driving a car, doing housework or talking on the phone, in a new and hopefully joyous way. I have included prayers that address emotional states that most of us experience, like waiting or worrying. I encourage you to also have a daily prayer time and have included suggestions for that as well. When you slowly incorporate some or all of these prayers, your life will become more peaceful and you will experience God's promise: "Come to me, all you who are weary and burdened, and I will give you rest" (Matthew 11:28-30 NIV). Your daily chores will become easier because they are infused with presence, and you will discover that even though you can't change some things in your life, you will be able to enjoy them more. Soon you will feel God's guidance in all of life and see the holy in the ordinary and the sacredness in all of creation.

My friend Ann's son, Frederick John Cox, died at the age of 27 in the 9/11 attack on the World Trade Center in New York City. His favorite quote was, "Do what you love; love what you do!" Though Freddy's life was taken at a tragically young age, he spent his years truly living! He celebrated each day and turned adversity into opportunity for growth. Let him be an inspiration for you, as he is for me, in our quest to do the same.

A Safe Place in God

God is a safe place to hide, ready to help when we need him.—
Psalm 46:1 (MSG)

Experiencing God as a safe place in our lives is what many of us need in this hectic and ever-changing world. There are so many demands placed on us that we often don't know which way to turn first or which task to check off the to-do list next. We are so caught up in our life situations that we hardly see the big picture anymore. God has a place for us to come to any time we need it!

When we pray from our safe place in God, we will develop the capacity to feel safe in all circumstances of life and know that true safety is not the absence of danger but the presence of God.

Although you are going within for a short period to "hide in God's safe place" during this prayer, it will heighten your awareness of safety and presence in your daily life. The withdrawal will help you to live more deeply in the present moment, because you will bring back the feeling of peace and safety. You can always withdraw to your safe place to pray because it is a place within and conducive to prayer.

God is our refuge and strength, an ever-present help in trouble.—Psalm 46:1 (NIV)

~ *Breathe slowly and let your thoughts wander to a place where you feel safe... Take your time and let an image of safety emerge from deep within... It might be a place in nature, in a house, on a boat or in a car... The place could be real or imagined...*

~ *Take your time and visualize the place in detail... What kind of light is in your safe place?... How is the temperature?... What do you hear?... What do you see?... What do you smell?... Visualize every detail of your safe place... How are you feeling?... Breathe gently and stay in your safe place for as long as you need...*

~ *Continue to breathe calmly and go back and forth between your present place and your safe place... Every time you go back and forth, you will bring the feeling of safety with you into the present moment... Keep the feeling of safety alive within you...*

~ *Gently rest in your breathing and know your safe place is within, and you can access it at any time... God's loving presence and protection is always with you.*

PRAYER: God is my safe place. Amen.

AWAKENING

This is the day the Lord has made; we will rejoice and be glad in it.—Psalm 118:24 (NKJV)

I chose the verb awakening rather than waking up, because if we start our waking up with prayer, we are not just waking up from a physical night's sleep but also from our spiritual dormancy – and we are all spiritually dormant in one way or another.

The moment we wake up and become conscious of the world, our hearts are still open to God. If we jump into our day without dedicating this pivotal moment to God, something life-giving will be lost. Beginning our day with God, we can trust "that all is well and all shall be well," as Julian of Norwich said in the fourteenth century.

Life is always changing and we don't really know what the new day will bring. Let us consecrate every new day by being aware of God's presence as the first thing we "do" and we will learn how to live above the circumstances of our lives. As a reminder to wake up slowly and attentively, you may want to hang something meaningful on the wall across from your bed.

Father in heaven! When the thought of thee wakes in our hearts, let it not awaken like a frightened bird that flies about in dismay, but like a child waking from its sleep with a heavenly smile.—Soren Kierkegaard (1813-1855)

~ *The moment you awaken, become aware of your breathing and your body... Stretch your body slowly and deliberately...*

~ *How are you feeling? Any wisdom God has laid upon your heart during the night?... Any dreams or insights?*

~ *Smile as you become fully awake and say inwardly or aloud, "This is the day the Lord has made; I will rejoice and be glad in it," or any other prayer that is meaningful to you...*

~ *Breathe deeply into the coming day, and know that life can only be lived one moment at a time. Awaken to the mystery of God in you each moment of your day.*

PRAYER: This is the day the Lord has made; I will rejoice and be glad in it. Amen.

Daily Prayer Time

Jesus said: "But you, when you pray, go into your inner room, close your door and pray to your Father who is in secret, and your Father who sees what is done in secret will reward you."—Matthew 6:6 (NASB)

All the prayers, except this one, are meant to be prayed while you are living your day and are reminders that while you are busy with what is going on in your daily life, God is always with you. I still want to encourage you to spend some time during your day exclusively with God. If we spend specific prayer time in God's presence, it will be so much easier to remember God throughout our busy days. Father Thomas Keating compares our relationship with God to friendship. If we don't spend quality time with a friend, we might lose the friendship after a while and we definitely are not nourished by it. Spending this time with God in whatever way speaks to you might save you time in the long run, because your decisions will be God-centered and you might save yourself from having to undo some poor choices.

I suggest you find a practice that works for you and stick with it every day. It is helpful to choose the same time and the same place. If you start with a ritual, perhaps lighting a candle, singing or listening to a certain song, it will add depth to your prayer time. It would be wonderful if you could arrange 20-30 minutes every day to dedicate to God alone, but if that feels stressful, you might want to begin with five or ten minutes. Praying regularly, if briefly, is much healthier than praying for long times but not being able to keep it up or enjoy it. Honestly assess your life and dedicate whatever time you can joyfully pray every day.

For those of you who already have a prayer ritual, you might want to learn about new forms of prayer or continue what you are already doing. And for those of you who would like to add a regular prayer time to your day, here are a few suggestions.

PRAYING PAUSE

> *"Don't pray when you feel like it. Have an appointment with the Lord and keep it."*—Corrie ten Boom (1892-1983)
>
> *Take a moment and meditate on the importance of this quote.*

If *devotional reading* works best for you, read daily devotions slowly and take some time to meditate on the words you read.

Lectio Divina is a prayer that is part of the Contemplative Christian tradition and comes from the Benedictines. You choose a Bible passage (most denominations have a daily lectionary) and read it very slowly a few times. When you read slowly, it is likely that a word, phrase or sentence will "jump" out at you. Ask yourself how it connects to your life and what God is telling you in these words. After you have meditated on it, pray to God about it, silently or aloud. Try it aloud and see how it feels. You might want to combine this prayer with journaling or writing a letter to God. Sit a few minutes in silence and give yourself completely to God. Write the word or phrase that spoke to you on a piece of paper and meditate on it throughout the day. It might connect you with something that happens during the day and help you to understand it in a Godly way. Lectio Divina can take five minutes to an hour depending on the time you can allow. Choose the amount of time that is right for you in this phase of your life. It's all good!

Centering Prayer is part of the Contemplative Christian tradition and it very simple but not easy. You sit in silence for 20 minutes (start with five minutes if that feels right for you) with your eyes closed or lowered. You choose a prayer word, which could be any word. I prefer a word that has a soothing and comforting meaning to me like "God," "Jesus," "Abba," "Be still," "Peace" or similar words. This word is your anchor in this prayer. When your mind strays away into the past or future, you gently guide yourself back into the presence of God and the present moment by inwardly saying your prayer word. I like to compare this way of praying to "Thy will be done" in the Lord's

Prayer. Every time I come back to my prayer word, I leave my thoughts behind (my will) and come back into the present moment with God (Thy will). This beautiful prayer might not feel like prayer at first but it will train your mind to stay in the presence of God at other times as well. Do not get frustrated when your mind wanders; it is part of this prayer! Be joyous that you discovered you strayed from "Thy will" and return to God's presence once more. When you have established a regular prayer practice, you might want to extend the period to 20 minutes.

Contemplative Outreach and Father Thomas Keating have developed the following guidelines:

1. Choose a sacred word as the symbol of your intention to consent to God's presence and action within.

2. Sitting comfortably and with eyes closed, settle briefly and silently introduce the sacred word as the symbol of your consent to God's presence and action within.

3. When engaged with your thoughts (thoughts include body sensations, feelings, images and reflections,) return ever-so-gently to the sacred word.

4. At the end of the prayer period, remain in silence with eyes closed for a couple of minutes."[5]

Driving a Car

In God we live and move and have our being.—Acts 17:28 (NIV)

Driving a car has become second nature to many of us. We get into the car and start driving without thinking about it. We know exactly what we have to do at a green light or stop sign, and we hit the brakes when we see the red brake lights of the car in front of us. We are often in a rush and eager to arrive somewhere, so we sacrifice the journey.

Many people use the time they spend driving to make phone calls and, by doing so, add another complex task to claim their attention. Let's remember that we are less likely to get in an accident when we are aware of our surroundings. If your mind is preoccupied with other things and places, it is as if you are driving the car from the passenger side. Let God be in the driver's seat of your life, "You're not in the driver's seat; I am" (Matthew 16:24 MSG) but stay in the driver's seat of your car.

Never drive faster than your guardian angel can fly.—Author Unknown

~ *When you get into your car, allow the rhythm of your breathing to calm you in body, mind and soul...*

~ *Become aware of your hands and rest both safely on the steering wheel... Be present in the car and know that God's presence is with you... If you are in a hurry, take an extra deep breath...*

~ *Now visualize yourself getting safely to the place you want to go...*

~ *Start the car and drive safely and alertly... Stay in the driver's seat, body, mind and soul...*

~ *At every red light, use the opportunity to pray... Be present in your environment...*

~ *Become aware that you will not arrive earlier by being tense and nervous...*

~ *When you get to your destination, thank God for your safe arrival and for protecting you and your loved ones.*

PRAYER: In God I live and move and have my being. Amen.

HOUSEWORK

Do everything readily and cheerfully – no bickering, no second-guessing allowed!... Provide people with a glimpse of good living and of the living God.—Philippians 2:14-15 (MSG)

Several disciplines in traditional Christian spirituality cultivate the awareness of God. The sacrament of the present moment is one of them. Let us celebrate life and the present moment and give people a glimpse of good living by doing our daily chores cheerfully around the house.

God is in the ordinary tasks of our lives as much as in our dedicated worship and prayer times. Changing our attitude and being grateful that we have dishes to wash, instead of complaining about having to wash them, will provide us "with a glimpse of good living and of the living God."

If we are aware of God in the small things of life, we then will be more likely to recognize God's hand in the big events of our lives.

I make this bed in the name of the Father, the Son and the Holy Spirit, in the name of the night I was conceived, in the name of the night I was born, in the name of the day I was baptized, in the name of each night, each day, each angel that is in the heavens.—Traditional Celtic prayer

~ *When you pick up a dish to be washed, come into the moment... There is no need to hurry... Look at the beauty of the dish and appreciate its color and form... Feel the warm water touch your skin as you rinse the dish...*

~ *When you prepare a meal, enjoy the colors of the fruits and vegetables and the smell of the bread... Feel the texture of the food you are preparing...*

~ *When you fold laundry, look at the colors, feel the fabric in your hands and breathe the smell of clean laundry... Think of the person it belongs to...*

~ *When you wash the floors, bathroom or kitchen counters, be grateful for these amenities in your life...*

~ *Provide people with a glimpse of good living and the living God by doing your daily chores cheerfully.*

PRAYER: I do my housework readily and cheerfully. Amen.

IN THE CHECKOUT LINE

Patience! You've got all the time in the world—whether a thousand years or a day, it's all the same to you.—Psalm 90:3 (NIV)

The grocery checkout line is the most wonderful place to practice the presence of God. Have you ever watched the lines and gone from one lane to the next because you thought it was faster just to discover that you would have been out the store had you stayed in the first one?

Patience! It won't go faster if you are impatient, nor will it make you happier if you get out the store faster. Your impatience will still be with you and you will rush to the next thing in life, missing life as you rush through it. If you accept that waiting in a checkout line is part of life, you will already be a happier person.

Practice patience the next time you go shopping, being present in your life, present to God and those God put in your path that day.

We have all the time in the world, time enough for life to unfold.—Louis Armstrong (1901-1971)

~ *When you stand in the checkout line and find yourself wondering whether this is the fastest lane, take a deep breath and stay in the lane you are in...*

~ *Be aware of your body and stand with your weight equally distributed on both feet... Relax your jaw, shoulders and stomach... Allow your breathing to calm and quiet your mind...*

~ *God is with you every moment... Be aware of the pure miracle of it... You are alive now...*

~ *Look around the store and appreciate everything you see, hear and feel... Be completely present and look at the people God put into your life in this moment... Smile... Talk to someone and make their day...*

~ *Be present and let God's patience and love flow through you into the world.*

PRAYER: I have all the time in the world. Amen.

LOOKING INTO THE MIRROR

For God made human beings in his own image.—Genesis 9:6 (NLT)

Many of us look into the mirror several times a day without really seeing ourselves. And if we do see ourselves, it is often with negative self-talk. We notice that our noses are too big, our eyes are too small, our hair doesn't have the right color or we are too heavy and getting old. Are you seeing yourself through negative, judgmental eyes?

There are three ways we can see ourselves: through our own eyes, the eyes of others, and through God's eyes. The first two are influenced by cultural norms that constantly change. The third one is the eternal unchanging truth!

When we love ourselves and focus on how God sees us, we are naturally beautiful, no matter what our appearance. We are as beautiful as we think we are.

Transform the moments you look into the mirror into moments of praise for God's miraculous creation and honor God by appreciating your beauty. Be patient with yourself because years of negative self-talk cannot be erased in an instant.

God created human beings; he created them godlike, reflecting God's nature.—Genesis 1:27 (MSG)

~ *When you stand in front of a mirror today, take a conscious breath and see what God sees...*

~ *Look at yourself as if you have never seen yourself before... Find a feature you do like in your face and know: God created you this way...*

~ *Find a feature you don't like in your face and know: God created you this way...*

~ *Hear God say, "You are my dearly beloved Son [Daughter], and you bring me great joy" (Mark 1:11 NLT). How does it feel to be this loved?...*

~ *Whenever you look in a mirror, pray this prayer of self-acceptance because you are made in the image of God. Praise God by letting God's beauty shine through you today.*

PRAYER: I am made in the image of God. Amen.

ON THE TELEPHONE

Oh Lord, open my lips and my mouth will declare your praise.—Psalm 51:15 (NIV)

With the invention of cell phones, we are able to make phone calls at the same time as driving a car, doing housework, walking the dog or watching the kids. It probably won't be difficult for you to add to this list. One of the saddest sights for me is watching a mom or dad on the playground playing with their kids while talking on the phone.

Many people are addicted to their cell phones – either talking, texting or checking their emails. Although we have all these devices to communicate in different ways, nothing can replace being with someone in person.

When your phone rings the next time, come into the present moment and be aware of the person on the other end. Whether this phone call will be a pleasant or unpleasant one, it will go infinitely better if you are aware that you are listening to one of God's children. Too often, we rush to the phone without taking a moment to relax and to be present. If you are the one making the call, be present and pray while you hear the ring tone.

Be impeccable with your word. Speak with integrity. Say only what you mean.—Miguel Ruiz

~ *When the phone rings, take a deep breath and become aware that someone is reaching out to you...*

~ *Take another deep breath and smile while you pick up the phone... When you smile, your voice will sound happy and the call will start on a wonderful note...*

~ *Throughout the conversation, be present and aware that you are talking to one of God's children... Listening to God involves more than your ears... It involves your heart and the ability to detach from your own agenda...*

~ *When you hang up, smile and thank God for the conversation.*

PRAYER: God, help me speak with love today. Amen.

OPENING A DOOR

I know your deeds. See, I have placed before you an open door that no one can shut.—Revelation 3:8 (NIV)

Do you know how many times during the day you open and close doors? It is one of those daily activities we do unconsciously. Take a moment and remember the times in your life when you stood before a closed door or the times when somebody left their door wide open for you. God's door is always open and no one can shut it, as the writer in Revelation promises. The real question is: Are you leaving the door open for God in your life?

Doors have a symbolic meaning in many cultures and religions. Opening a door symbolizes a new beginning while closing a door means leaving something behind. A door can also be seen as a transition from one passage of life into another and a threshold where two worlds come together.

When one door of happiness closes, another opens; but often we look so long at the closed door that we do not see the one which has been opened for us.—Helen Keller (1880-1968)

~ *Become aware of the times you open or close a door...
You might want to put a sticky note on the door as a
reminder to pray...*

~ *When you open a door, you might want to say, "I am
opening this door into the presence of God." Or, "I am
opening this door to love, forgiveness, kindness,
peace, joy" or whatever positive force you would like
to welcome into your life...*

~ *If you want to be more specific, the act of opening a
door could be an opportunity to say a specific prayer
to God. "Please, God, open the door to health for my
loved one," or "Please, God, open this door to love in
my life"...*

~ *When you close a door, you might want to say, "I am
closing the door to hatred, greed, judgment, the pain
of the past" or whatever it is you want to give up in
your life...*

~ *May every door you are not meant to walk through
be shut, and every door that leads to God be opened.*

PRAYER: God's door is always open. Amen.

RESTING IN GOD

Come to me, all you who are weary and burdened, and I will give you rest.—Matthew 11:28(NIV)

Resting in God is one of the most wonderful and difficult things to do. Let us take a break from our stress-filled agendas and take this invitation from Jesus seriously. God rested on the seventh day. When have you last rested for a whole day and honored a holy day per week?

Even though it might be difficult for many of us to rest a whole day, we can still follow Jesus' invitation and take a few minutes every day and "rest in God." It will not only deepen our relationship with God, but also benefit our life, our work and our health.

Neurological research has shown that tensing and relaxing the body is beneficial for people who are unusually tense. It is effective in reducing stress and anxiety; helping with pain, heart disease and other neurological, psychological and physical disorders; and is as effective as taking sleep-inducing medications when practiced at night. It also helps people to relax before operations and aids in postoperative recovery.

Rest in Me, My weary one, for this is a form of worship.
—Sarah Young

~ *Lie down on a carpet, yoga mat, or outside in the grass if possible. If lying down is not a possibility, simply sit in a chair and become aware of your breath...*

~ *Breathe in, hold your breath and tense your face... Breathe out and relax. Repeat this rhythm and tense your arms ... your stomach ... your legs while holding your breath and relax while you are breathing out...*

~ *Now tense all the muscles in your body at once, from head to toe, and hold the tension as long as possible. On a spiritual level it represents "your will" working in you...*

~ *As you breathe out, relax your body completely into the floor or chair... Feel your body... On a spiritual level this represents "God's will" working in you... Repeat relaxing and tensing your body several times...*

~ *Are you more relaxed and peaceful? Slowly get up and remember to rest in God throughout the day.*

PRAYER: I rest in God. Amen.

SUNRISE

From the rising of the sun to its setting the name of the Lord is to be praised.—Psalm 113:3 (NRSV)

The glory of a sunrise is beyond words and to praise God's name while watching it comes naturally. Every sunrise is different and still beautiful. Some mornings the sky is clear and the sunrise is completely visible from its first red glow to its full round beauty. Other mornings it is cloudy and the sun peeks out behind a layer of clouds and goes back into another layer as soon as it has risen. Sometimes the sky is completely overcast and the sun cannot be seen at all.

The sunrise is a lovely metaphor for God's work in our lives. Sometimes we can see it clearly, while at other times it is hidden behind a cloud of pain, to reveal itself when we least expect it. As surely as we know that the sun rises every day, we can also be sure that God is present in our lives every moment whether we can feel it or not.

A wonderful gift you can give to yourself and God is to get up before dawn once in a while and watch the darkness turn into light.

Glory to thee, Thou glorious sun, Face of the God of life.
—Traditional Celtic prayer

~ *If possible, get up early once in a while to experience the rise of a new day, and walk or drive to a place in nature where you can see the sun rise and the night turn into day...*

~ *If you have to stay at home, sit by a window and see the world come into focus with the coming of the daylight...*

~ *Breathe, watch and listen, and receive the spirit of dawn... Let your thoughts be asleep a little longer and let your senses be awake...*

~ *This beautiful nature experience happens every day without fail and we can choose to be a part of it every day just as we can choose to be aware of God's presence every moment of the day.*

PRAYER: I am awake to God's glory. Amen.

Turning on the Light

You are the light of the world... let your light shine before others, that they may see your good deeds and glorify your Father in heaven.—Matthew 5:14-15 (NIV)

Upon entering a dark room, we switch on the light. Most of the time we do it unconsciously because it is such a common activity. Have you ever stopped and thought about how miraculous it is to be able to turn on a light switch and bring light into a dark room?

This is a wonderful metaphor for our life in the Spirit. If you practice the Prayers of Presence daily, they will become a part of you and your life will be illumined by the prayers. Praying this particular prayer will affect your self-esteem in several ways. You will become more confident and let "your light" shine in ever deeper ways.

The smallest light dispels darkness, and through the smallest prayer, God brings light into our lives. If you take this "mini retreat" every night becoming aware that all light is God's light, you will not only lose your fear of the physical darkness, but of the darkness in life.

Our deepest fear is not that we are inadequate... It is our light, not our darkness, that most frightens us... We were born to make manifest the glory of God that is within us.
—Marianne Williamson

~ *When you touch the light switch to turn on the light, become aware of this small but metaphorically powerful transformation...*

~ *Switch on the light and breathe into the knowledge that you are God's light in this world...*

~ *Hear Jesus say your name and, "You are the light of the world," or say to yourself, "I am the light of the world"...*

~ *Continue your evening with the knowledge that God's light shines within you...*

~ *When you turn off the light, know that God's light is always with you.*

PRAYER: I am the light of the world. Amen.

WAITING

Be still before the LORD and wait patiently for him.—Psalm 37:7-8 (NIV)

We often "can't wait" for something to happen. We say, "I can't wait until the weekend..." or "I can't wait for this time of my life to be over..." and we miss our life altogether.

Another way we don't like to wait is at a red light, in a traffic jam, or at a doctor's office. What these moments have in common is a dislike for our present situation and we wish our precious time away.

"Be still before the Lord" is a different kind of waiting. Sometimes we have to wait after we have planted the seeds in our lives, as Jesus tells us in the parable of the sower (Mark 4:26-29). There's a beautiful story about a man who is so eager to "help" a butterfly into the world that he opens its chrysalis. The result is tragic: the wings of the butterfly don't develop properly and it can never fly. Though the tale of the butterfly is very sad, it provides a concrete metaphor that encourages us to await God's perfect timing with confidence.

God grant me the serenity to accept the things I cannot change; courage to change the things I can; and the wisdom to know the difference.—Reinhold Niebuhr (1892-1971)

~ When you are waiting for a life circumstance to change, whether it be an illness or a painful emotional situation and you feel powerless to change it, know that God is at work in you, "drying your wings"...

~ Remember the times when, as a child, you were waiting for Christmas to arrive, enjoying the excitement of the time of waiting, knowing that Christmas would come. Learn to wait on God this way and know that God uses everything for good...

~ Use a time of waiting to worship God in whatever way feels right for you; pray your favorite Breath Prayer, slowly pray the Lord's Prayer or smile and connect with the people who are waiting with you...

~ When you are waiting in line, breathe deeply and look around you. God is present in everything you see and hear...

~ Savor the pure miracle of being alive! Enjoy life! You are only alive this moment and God is alive in you!

PRAYER: I wait patiently before the Lord. Amen.

WORRYING

Therefore do not worry about tomorrow, for tomorrow will worry about itself. Each day has enough trouble of its own.— Matthew 6:34 (NIV)

When we worry, we practice the absence of God rather than the presence of God. Worrying only happens for future events because when we assess challenges to come, we measure the future and its tasks with the strength God has given us for today. We forget that we will have as much or more strength as we need when we need it. The amount we worry could be a measurement for how much faith we have in God. If we worry a lot, it really means that we have little faith in God's strength and are relying on our own. There is not only a connection between worrying and faith but also between God's blessings and faith. The more we trust God, the more blessings we will be able to receive because we are opening up to God's provision and plan and not our own.

Let's stay in the present moment and ask for God's help and trust that God will give us what we need day by day to live a joyous and productive life.

"For I know the plans I have for you," declares the Lord, "plans to prosper you and not to harm you, plans to give you hope and a future."—Jeremiah 29:11 (NIV)

~ *Whenever you find yourself worrying, take a deep breath and look around... What do you see?... What do you hear?*

~ *Take another deliberate breath and look back on a situation where you worried and God worked everything out better than you could have imagined. Draw strength and faith from that memory and know that God will come through for you again...*

~ *As you continue to breathe deliberately and deeply, calming body, mind and soul, pray a short prayer like "Be still and know that I am God," "For I know the plans I have for you," or any other short prayer and repeat it until it you are calmer...*

~ *Feel the love God has for you and continue your day in the assurance that God is taking care of you moment by moment.*

PRAYER: In God I trust. Amen.

NOTES

PREFACE

1. Richard Rohr, *The Naked Now: Learning to See as the Mystics See* (New York: Crossroad, 2009), 23.

PART I

The Christian Foundation of the Prayers of Presence

1. Brother Lawrence, Introduction and Notes by Tony Jones, *Practicing the Presence of God* (Brewster: Paraclete Press, 2007), 93.
2. Ibid., 64.
3. Brother Lawrence, *The Practice of the Presence of God and the Spiritual Maxims* (Mineola: Dover Publications, 2005), 38.
4. Ibid., 50.
5. Ibid., 75.
6. Ibid., 54.
7. Ibid., 59.
8. Ibid., 45.
9. Ibid., 62.
10. Ibid., 10.
11. Ibid., 16.
12. Ibid.
13. Ibid., 7.
14. Ibid., 31.
15. Ibid., 47.
16. Ibid.
17. Ibid., 30.

18. Macrina Wiederkehr, *A Tree Full of Angels: Seeing the Holy in the Ordinary* (San Francisco: Harper Collins, 1990), 57.
19. Anonymous, *The Cloud of Unknowing* (New York: Doubleday, 1973), 84.
20. Lawrence, *The Practice of the Presence of God and the Spiritual Maxims,* 50.
21. Ibid.
22. Ibid., 22.
23. Anthony de Mello. *One Minute Wisdom,* (India: Gujarat, 1985), 11.

The Physical and Neurological Effect of the Prayers of Presence

1. Jill Bolte Taylor, *My Stroke of Insight: A Brain Scientist's Personal Journey* (New York: Penguin, 2009), 44.
2. Ibid., 41.
3. Ibid., 42-43.
4. Ibid., 29.
5. Ibid., 30.
6. Ibid., 29.
7. Ibid., 159.
8. Ibid., 168.
9. Ibid., 168-184.
10. Ibid., 174.
11. Andrew Newberg/Mark Robert Waldman, *How God Changes Your Brain* (New York: Random House, 2009), 174.
12. Ibid., 17.
13. Ibid., 7.
14. Ibid., 8.

15. Ibid., 15.
16. Ibid., 149-169.
17. Ibid., 163.
18. Ibid.
19. Ibid., 170.
20. Ibid.
21. Ibid., 175.
22. Ibid.

The Psychological and Emotional Effect of the Prayers of Presence

1. http://biblesuite.com/greek/4336.htm (accessed November 14, 2013).
2. Richard Rohr, *Breathing Under Water: Spirituality and the Twelve Steps* (Cincinnati: St. Anthony Messenger Press, 2011), 96-97.
3. Rohr, *The Naked Now*, 23.
4. Frederick Buechner, *Telling Secrets: A Memoir* (New York: HarperCollins, 1991), 104.
5. Lawrence/Jones, 51.
6. Ibid., 109.
7. Keating, Thomas, *Open Mind, Open Hear: The Contemplative Dimension of the Gospel* (New York: The Continuum Publishing Group, 2003), 13-15.
8. Taylor, 29.
9. Lawrence/Jones, 22.
10. Margaret Guenther, *My Soul in Silence Waits: Meditations on Psalm 62* (Boston: Cowley, 2000), 119.
11. Newberg/Waldman, 5.
12. Ibid., inside cover.
13. Ibid., 104.

14. Ibid., 67-146.

15. Ibid., 82.

16. Ibid., 68.

17. Lawrence/Jones, 51.

18. Newberg/Waldman, 88.

19. Ibid., 90.

20. Guenther, 58.

21. Ibid., 62.

22. St. John of the Cross, quoted in: Cynthia Bourgeault, *Centering Prayer and Inner Awakening* (Cambridge: Cowley, 2004), 7.

23. Thomas Hart, *Hidden Spring: The Spiritual Dimension of Therapy* (Minneapolis: Augsburg Fortress, 2002), 47.

24. Buechner, *Telling Secrets*, 105.

25. Taylor, 168.

26. John O'Donohue, *Anam Cara: A Book of Celtic Wisdom* (New York: HarperCollins, 1998), 177.

Practicing the Prayers of Presence

1. Anita Moorjani, *Dying to Be Me: My Journey from Cancer to Near Death to True Healing* (Carlsbad: Hay House, 2012), 160.

2. David Frenette, *The Path of Centering Prayer: Deepening Your Experience of God* (Boulder: Sounds True, 2012), 198.

3. Eckhart Tolle, *Practicing the Power of Now: Essential Teachings, Meditations, and Exercises from the Power of Now* (Novato: New World Library, 1999), 119.

4. Anthony de Mello, *The Song of the Bird* (New York: Doubleday, Image Books edition, 1984), 67-68.

5. Wayne Mueller, *Legacy of the Heart: The Spiritual Advantages of a Painful Childhood* (New York: Simon & Schuster, 1992), 67.

6. Frenette, 140.

7. Ibid., 154.

8. Ibid., 132.

9. Lawrence, *The Practice of the Presence of God and the Spiritual Maxims,* 47.

10. Ibid., 22.

PART II

The Breath Prayers
1. Rohr, *The Naked Now,* 25.
2. Newberg/Waldman, 184
3. Frenette, 53.
4. Newberg/Waldman, 179.

The Body Awareness Prayers
1. O'Donohue, 47.
2. Buechner, *Telling Secrets,* 83.
3. O'Donohue, 58.

The Daily Awareness Prayers
1. Frederick Buechner, *Wishful Thinking: A Theological ABC* (New York: HarperCollins, 1993), 119.
2. Kent Nerburn, *Small Graces: The Quiet Gifts of Everyday Life* (Novato: New World Library, 1998), 11.
3. Tolle, 31.

4. Paula D'Arcy, *Gift of the Red Bird:. The Story of a Divine Encounter,* (New York: Crossroad Publishing, 1996), 95.

5. http://www.contemplativeoutreach.org/category/category/ centering-prayer, "Method of Centering Prayer" (accessed November 14, 2013.

GRATITUDE

No man is an island. - Thomas Merton (1915-1958)

It takes a village to raise a child and a lot of friends and family to publish a book.

My friend Ann Douglas planted the seed for this book while we were driving back from a retreat in southern Georgia. Years later at another retreat (when I was working on the book), I told the story of my grandfather-in-law Simon Schuller shouting, "This is living!" while he enjoyed a cup of coffee or saw a beautiful flower in his yard. Ann beamed and exclaimed, *"This is Living! Practicing the Presence of God."* I knew instantly this was the title for my book. Thank you, Ann!

My friend Gina White watered the "book seed" by asking whether I had ever thought of publishing my prayers as a book. Gina had been ill for a long time and needed meditative prayers to keep her connected with God. When she asked me to write the prayers down for her, one cornerstone for this book was laid with love for a dear friend. Gina also painted the beautiful painting for the cover of this book. Thank you, Gina!

After I had written the first chapter on Brother Lawrence, I gave it to my daughter Maya who was in college at the time majoring in "Editing, Writing and Media." Maya called me and said, "Mami, this is the first time I understand the concept of living in the present moment with God." Maya supported me with her editing skills and unwavering love for this book throughout the whole process. Thank you, Maya!

My niece Carolin Proeger, a graphic designer, not only created the cover for this book but the website as well. Her supportive daily texts from Germany and her enthusiasm in helping me to publish and market my book meant the world to me. Thank you, Carolin!

I can surely say that this book would not have been published if it weren't for the support and help of my friend Liz Stiles. In her loving way, she kept on nudging and encouraging me and tirelessly worked on the formatting of the manuscript. Her enthusiasm and hard work kept me going through the tedious steps of publishing *This is Living!* Thank you, Liz!

Many other friends and retreat participants read the manuscript and encouraged me to publish the book. They also inspired me by letting me know how much the prayers had helped them. Thank you to all of you! You are too many to name and you know how grateful I am.

Thank you for bringing God into my daily life by letting me know I was loved when I most needed it.

About the Author

 Bettina Schuller is a native of Germany and has lived in the United States since 1989. She attended the University of Bremen in Germany and earned a master's degree in special education. Her teaching career evolved into becoming a teacher for Centering Prayer. Bettina studied spirituality at both the School of Theology at the University of the South in Sewanee, Tennessee, and the Episcopal Divinity School in Cambridge, Massachusetts. She is a certified spiritual director and leads retreats in Canada and the United States. Helping spiritual seekers live in the present moment and listen to the "still, small voice" within is the main focus of her work. Bettina is the mother of two daughters and lives in St. Petersburg, Florida.

Bettina can be reached at www.bettinaschuller.com.